# Charlie Tully

## CELTIC'S CHEEKY CHAPPIE

# Charlie Tully

## CELTIC'S CHEEKY CHAPPIE

TOM CAMPBELL

breedon **books**
PUBLISHING

First published in Great Britain in 2008 by

The Breedon Books Publishing Company Limited

Breedon House, 3 The Parker Centre,

Derby, DE21 4SZ.

ISBN: 978-1-85983-670-5

Printed and bound by Cromwell Press, Trowbridge, Wiltshire.

# Contents

Acknowledgements                                                      6
They said it…                                                         7
Foreword by Billy McNeill                                             9
Preface                                                              10

1  The Case for Canonisation                                         12
2  First-hand Recollections                                          24
3  Baptism(s)                                                        38
4  Life Before Glasgow                                               45
5  Sudden Impact                                                     56
6  The Worst of Times                                                74
7  The Scottish Cup – At Last                                        90
8  An Antic Disposition                                              96
9  Celtic's Achilles Heel                                           107
10 A Luxury Player?                                                  116
11 One-offs                                                          127
12 Breakthrough!                                                     135
13 The Last Hurrah – and the Greatest                               145
14 Rangers and Other Opponents                                      158
15 The End in Glasgow                                               170
16 When the Cheering Stops                                          181
17 The Road All Runners Come                                        201
18 The Real Charlie Tully                                           204

*Appendices*                                                        **216**
Tullyisms                                                           216
The Flag Flutter                                                    218
Full Circle                                                         221
Last Word                                                           223

# Acknowledgements

I am deeply indebted to the following for all their help, freely and willingly given, and for material generously loaned:

Charlie Tully's children – Charlie Jr, Patricia (Conlon) and Brian; his brother Billy; the eminent journalists and football men – Malcolm Brodie in Belfast and Bob Crampsey in Glasgow; the 'Celtic men' – Pat Woods and Frank Glencross for proofreading the manuscript and gently pointing out the error of my ways, and for providing photographs and other valuable background material; Billy McNeill for providing a professional's insight into Charlie Tully's character, and for writing the foreword; Sean Fallon for sharing his memories of his countryman; Johnny Paton for recalling in such detail the 1948–49 season as his left-wing partner; Tom McGrath for giving permission to reproduce his famous poem about the footballer; Phil Freeman of Liverpool University for reading the manuscript and suggesting improvements; Padraig Coyle for providing details of Charlie Tully's later career in Ireland; Senga Fairgrieve for turning the raw material into a form acceptable to the publisher; and to all at Breedon for their professionalism, patience and understanding in producing the book.

# They said it...

'Charlie Tully? Totally different class. A player who never wasted a ball, and who was always thinking ahead. To be frank, we were not always smart enough to anticipate what he might do.'

**Willie Fernie**

'A Jack the Lad in the best sense of the expression, not a malicious bone in his body. Impish.'

**Padraig Coyle**

'There was always somebody in the house. The craic was great. My father was always happy staying up late, talking and singing. He could put a song together.'

**Patricia Conlon**

'My da was never a materialistic person. For example, he used to have his souvenirs — medals, caps, jerseys etc — lying around the house. Some in a drawer, others in a shoe-box. He never put them on display nor made a shrine out of them. He knew everybody and everybody knew him, and many people would tap him for money. He was generous to a fault. Once, when he was short himself, and that happened sometimes, he gave away one of his medals to an acquaintance in Glasgow and told him to get what he could for it. The man, of course, took it to a pawnshop...but the pawnbroker examined the medal and contacted Celtic Park. An official came round to the pawnshop, redeemed the medal for cash, and Charlie was summoned to the ground. He was given a *lecture and a slap on the wrist but also his medal back. Charlie told the family that he repeated this formula later with his "dependant" a number of times…but we all knew he was kidding (at least we thought he was kidding), but you could never tell with Charlie Tully.'*

**Brian Tully**

'*Charlie Tully? Often enough the facts came close to equalling the myth; sometimes they surpassed them.'*

**Bob Crampsey**

'*Never mind the truth! Print the legend.'*

**Advice to the author**

# *Foreword*

I have been a Celtic supporter all my life, I suppose, but I was always too busy playing football as a boy to see too many games. The first one I remember seeing was Celtic against Aberdeen around 1949, when I was a wee boy of 10. My Auntie Grace took me to Celtic Park on a supporters' bus from Bellshill. It was a miserable wet afternoon, the pitch was heavy and muddy…and Celtic were poor throughout the first half. And then Charlie Tully took over. He was up against a fearsome-looking full-back in Don Emery, but he ran him ragged and helped Celtic score three times in the last 15 minutes to win by 4–2. From that moment on, Charlie Tully was my favourite player. To be perfectly honest, he was everybody's favourite player.

In the 1940s Celtic were in the doldrums, but Charlie Tully changed all that; the team started to win things, the crowds came back. He did a great deal to lift the spirits of people who had endured the hardships of World War Two and the austerity of Britain for years after it. Charlie was a breath of fresh air: a clever player, a superb entertainer, and he brought the crowds back to Celtic Park. He had talent to spare and football intelligence in abundance. And he was a character on and off the pitch.

I first met him when I was a young player with Celtic and he was nearing the end of his career. But he was still Charlie Tully: player and entertainer, and also a man who loved life and football. He lived for playing football and matching talent and wits against opponents. At training he was friendly and approachable, always ready for a laugh. For him, life was a ball to be enjoyed by everybody and shared with everybody.

I remember him as a great player who brightened life for Celtic supporters in a grim time and as a man who lived life to the full, loving what he did. He deserves to be remembered as a player, as a character and as a true Celtic legend.

*Billy McNeill*

# *Preface*

Charlie Tully's name continues to reverberate around Celtic Park on match days, chanted by thousands who are clearly too young ever to have seen him play.

*Oh, they gave us James McGrory and Paul McStay,*
*Johnstone, Tully, Murdoch, Auld and Hay,*
*And most of football's greats have passed through Parkhead's gates,*
*To play the game the Glasgow Celtic way.*

Tully came to Glasgow in 1948, a local hero in Belfast but untested in the harder, more professional world of Scottish football. Within four years, this young man's impact had made his a household name and virtually guaranteed his inclusion in any future Celtic Hall of Fame. What had he done to merit such a reputation? For one thing, he had helped Celtic out of what must have seemed to the supporters a terminal decline. These football doldrums had lasted throughout World War Two and lingered on for three seasons after the conflict; indeed, only a month or so before Charlie Tully joined Celtic, the famed Parkhead club were slipping to the brink of relegation. The young Irishman brought with him the promise of better days. His talent and skill astonished and delighted a generation of Celtic followers brought up on bland fare served up by journeymen, and his cheek and imagination added entertainment value to an austere post-war football scene.

Long before the word had become debased, Charles Patrick Tully was a 'celebrity' – one of the first footballers to earn the description. In 1948, only a few weeks after his arrival, he almost single-handedly ran Rangers' famous 'Iron Curtain' defence ragged in a memorable 3–1 win for Celtic at Parkhead in the League Cup. In 1949, in the infamous

Cox—Tully incident at Ibrox Park, he was the innocent victim of an assault that precipitated a near-riot, in which scores of spectators were injured and arrests made. Later in the same season, he joked with the zany American comedian Danny Kaye in front of 80,000 at Hampden Park, prior to leading Celtic to a 3–2 victory over Rangers in the Charity Cup Final. In 1950 – a Holy Year – along with the rest of the Celtic party, he had met Pope Pius XII in an audience at St Peter's in Rome, a few days before playing against Lazio in the Italian club's Golden Jubilee celebrations. On the Channel crossing from Dover to Ostend, he made a great impression on a fellow traveller, the legendary crooner and film star Bing Crosby, with whom he chatted (and probably drank a pint or two). In 1951, fresh from winning the Scottish Cup after beating Motherwell 1–0, Charlie and his Celtic team were mobbed and welcomed home from a tour of the United States by a crowd of more than 5,000 at the Central Station. In 1952, while playing for Northern Ireland, he scored both goals in a 2–2 draw against a powerful England side. One of the goals came direct from a corner-kick, which completely bamboozled Gil Merrick in the English goal, and this was after promising England's right-back, Alf Ramsey, he would 'roast' him. And there would be more, so much more to Charles Patrick Tully, who developed into a star player in his 11 seasons with Celtic. He was a genuine celebrity and – in the hyperbole of sports writers – a legend.

Whenever I mentioned to anybody that I was writing a book about Charlie Tully, the reaction was always the same: a smile, a momentary silence in which memories came flooding back and the shake of the head, 'Oh that Charlie Tully! What a character, and a player too!' Anybody who earned such a reputation as a player – and who brought smiles to faces – deserves to be remembered.

# Chapter 1
## ———— *The Case for Canonisation* ————

It is a matter of considerable regret that the one indelible action of Charlie Tully, imprinted in the minds (if not the memory) of all Celtic supporters, was not captured on camera to verify once and for all what exactly happened that day – 21 February 1953. The occasion was a third-round Scottish Cup tie between Falkirk and Celtic at Brockville Park, before a record crowd of 23,100.

Poems would be written about it, including this one by Tom McGrath:

> *there was that time charlie tully*
>
> *took a corner kick*
>
> *an' you know how he*
>
> *wus always great at taking thaem*
>
> *tae curve in, well charlie takes the corner*
>
> *and it curved in and fuck me did the wind*
>
> *no cerry it right intae the net. but they*
>
> *disputed it. and the linesman hud the*
>
> *flag up and they goat away wae it and tully*
>
> *hud tae take it again. an fuck me does he no get*
>
> *it in the net again. you should have*
>
> *seen it. it just seemed to go roon*
>
> *in a kind o' hauf circle. above aw their*
>
> *heids. Fucking keeper didnae know where tae look…*

As a match report, the work fails miserably; as a poem, it succeeds splendidly. The poet is deliberately vague regarding details of time and place. The occasion, the venue, the opponents and even Tully's own team are not mentioned. The overall impression is of one central character — a solitary hero and mythic figure — emerging from the mists of folk-memory and concentrating on fulfilling a quest, facing a challenge and succeeding in it, despite overwhelming odds. All is described in the words of the common man, who voices his admiration and awestruck disbelief in the coarse language of the terracing. Most significantly, no details of Charlie Tully are provided. He is a name only, and it is to be assumed that everybody knows exactly who 'Charlie Tully' is. And quite rightly.

Tom McGrath, a distinguished Scottish poet, was born in Rutherglen in 1940 and is a Celtic supporter. Charlie Tully, he claims, was his favourite player — 'a supreme entertainer'. He also thinks he saw Tully score this famous corner-kick but, in a conversation with the author, felt that it was at Celtic Park; he states categorically that he has never been to Brockville in his life. I would suggest that this confirms the mythic stature of Charlie Tully, whereby even honest men remain confused by what they saw or did not see.

* * *

Joe Devers, a lifetime Celtic fan, was home on leave from his national service in Shropshire with the Royal Artillery when he attended the match with the author. This is his memory of the event:

*To judge by the number of people who swear that they were at Hampden for the League Cup Final when Celtic beat Rangers 7–1, probably there were about 150,000 Celtic supporters present that afternoon. Too bad that the official attendance that day was announced at 82,293!...Similarly, so many chapels in the Middle Ages claimed to have a fragment of the True Cross that cynics estimated that Jesus must have been crucified on a cross 40ft by 30...But I can swear to this: that I was there in Falkirk for a Scottish Cup match when Charlie Tully scored with two corner-kicks — and not only was I there but I was within a few yards of Tully when he took the corners! I saw the miracle with my own eyes...I remember several things about that game: Celtic were two goals down very early and were being played off the pitch by Falkirk, who were winning every 50–50 ball. Celtic's defence looked shaky and could have given up a couple of other goals before half-time. When the whistle went at the end of the first half, Celtic were booed off the pitch by their own supporters...Everything changed about five minutes into the second half. Celtic had scarcely mounted a single attack, but they did win a corner on the left at the Railway End of the ground. Brockville was packed that day. I was in the covered enclosure, right at the front and within yards of the corner flag. There was no running track at Brockville, I remember, and you were so close you could reach out and touch the players when they took a throw-in...Back to the corner-kick. Tully placed the ball for the kick but put it outside the arc. Not very much, but it was clear enough. I had seen him doing this several times before in other matches, and I think he did it to wind up the opposition. At Brockville that day, he had the excuse that he could hardly take a step backward because the Celtic supporters at that end of the ground had come over the wall to perch even closer to the pitch, such was the overcrowding...At any rate, Tully took the kick with his right foot, an inswinger. At first I thought it was too low, that the full-back at the post could clear it with his head, but the ball swerved and went straight* into the net. The Falkirk goalkeeper was stationed at the back post and did not have time to reach the ball...Celebrations! Tully with his arms in the air at the corner flag – and hundreds of Celtic supporters around him, jumping up and down...Thousands of others poured on to the pitch dancing with joy and prancing around. The man beside me had the weatherbeaten face of somebody who had seen it all before in a lifetime of following Celtic. Once he had recovered a bit, he nodded sagely and said to me 'That's it, son. Celtic'll go on to win after that'...But the linesman way up the pitch was signalling furiously. I knew right away what it was: he must have had a perfect view of where Tully had placed the ball, and he wanted to speak to the referee. The conversation took place right in front of me, and you didn't need to be a lip-reader to guess what was being said. Finally the referee indicated that the 'goal' was being disallowed and that the corner had to be retaken. Anger among the Celtic hordes behind that goal, celebration among the home supporters – and relief for the Falkirk players. Tully was raging, but he was totally in the wrong. He argued with the referee and the linesman but eventually accepted the situation and started to place the ball within the arc. He straightened up and called the referee over, insisting that he had no room now for a run-up if the ball was placed correctly; the referee had stationed himself for the corner-kick and had to move about 20 yards towards Tully to speak to him. Tully shrugged his shoulders, shook his head in frustration and, believe it or not, he handed the ball to the linesman to place for him. I was there, remember, and I saw it with my own eyes and I am an honest man...Several minutes had gone by, and the crowd were excited – a bit too much, I thought. At last Tully took the kick, a little bit higher this time. Another inswinger, and the full-back on the line at the post had no chance of reaching it. The goalkeeper was a bit late in reacting to the swerve on the ball, and it deceived him completely too. I *don't think he got a touch on that ball…Absolute pandemonium this time. Again Tully disappeared into the crowd, again the spectators poured on to the pitch. On the terracing behind them you could see that some of the safety barriers had snapped under the pressure and were twisted out of shape. It was becoming frightening, I can tell you…The old man beside me must have been the coolest man in Brockville that day. Again he nodded and shook his head, unsurprised: 'I told you, son, Celtic can't lose now'…He was right, of course. Falkirk just collapsed after that, and Celtic got another two goals to win comfortably in the end. Celtic, through to the next round of the Cup, were cheered off the pitch, a real change from half-time. Quite a game, and I was there! They say that it requires two miracles for the church to recognise somebody as a saint; well, Charlie performed two that day, and there were quite a few witnesses present to prove it.*

\* \* \*

The poet, Tom McGrath, has had his moment and the supporter, Joe Devers, has had the chance to give his opinion. It is now time for the historian to add the specifics and perhaps, in view of Joe's closing words, act as a sort of devil's advocate. The line up was as follows:

**Falkirk:** McFeat, McDonald, Rae, Gallagher, McKenzie, Hunter, Delaney, Dunlop, Weir, Campbell, Brown.

**Celtic:** Bonnar, Haughney, Meechan, Evans, Stein, McPhail, Collins, Walsh, McGrory, Fernie, Tully.

A Celtic defeat at Brockville that day (21 February 1953) would not have been a great shock. Celtic were struggling in the League, mired in mid-table, halfway through an inconsistent season and with a side unsettled in formation and personnel. Several journalists sensed that underdogs Falkirk, eager for glory in the Scottish Cup and playing at home on a narrow pitch in winter conditions, could provide such an upset. The police authorities had decreed that the Cup tie should be all-ticket with a limit of 23,100 – a record crowd for Brockville. But 30 minutes before the kick-off, parts of the ground already appeared dangerously overcrowded, especially behind the goal at the Railway End, an area almost totally filled with Celtic supporters, and the crowds were still pouring in.

Two players in the dark blue of Falkirk were very familiar to Celtic followers: Jimmy Delaney and Jock Weir. In 1953 Delaney, one of the most popular players ever to wear a Celtic jersey, was scarcely a potent force at the age of 38 (he had won a Scottish Cup medal with Celtic in 1937); Weir, a bustling whole-hearted forward, had played himself into the Celtic histories with three goals against Dundee at Dens Park on the last day of the 1947–48 season, staving off the threat of relegation. The fact that both players, clearly past their best, still featured in Falkirk's line up was yet another indication that the Bairns were the underdogs.

Despite the bitterly cold weather, the pitch was heavy and holding rather than frozen and icy, but the players still moved cautiously in their warm-ups. Falkirk roared into action straight from the kick-off, and Celtic were immediately put on the defensive. Delaney was their main concern as he repeatedly skipped past Meechan, who had to resort to rugged tackling to stop the sprightly veteran. His tackling gave several dangerous free-kicks to Falkirk and seemed designed to slow down Delaney or to intimidate him into subjugation. Meechan's tactics raised the ire of the Falkirk supporters in the stand and promoted mixed reactions among many in Celtic's travelling support, who still revered Jimmy Delaney as an all-time Celtic hero.

To nobody's great surprise, Jock Weir gave Falkirk the lead after five minutes. The only player to react to a bouncing ball in Celtic's penalty area, and totally unmarked within the six-yard box, Weir's header beat an immobile John Bonnar in Celtic's goal. Celtic's defenders glared at each other, no doubt very conscious that the stocky Weir had scored very few goals with his head throughout his career. Worse was to follow when Campbell scored a second goal in 18 minutes. The ball broke towards the inside-left in a packed goalmouth, again without any effective challenge from the surrounding defenders. Falkirk's support, almost doubled in numbers for this Cup tie, erupted into raucous delight; Celtic's lapsed into a sullen discontent.

At half-time, Falkirk left the pitch to a standing ovation, while Celtic left with the boos from their own supporters ringing in their ears. Even Charlie Tully had been totally ineffective, scarcely touching the ball in that first half. In fact, several times he had been caught in possession amid groans of disapproval from Celtic's legions. His first contribution, within seconds of the restart, was also an unfortunate one. Delaney, Falkirk's outside-right, and Tully, Celtic's outside-left, passed each other in opposite directions, and Tully elbowed Falkirk's talisman as they passed. John McPhail, Celtic's left-half, who had played with Delaney during the wartime seasons as a teenager, sportingly patted the outraged veteran on the shoulder – but it was a moment to remember with distaste. Not a brutal foul but an unacceptable action, it provided evidence of the irritating side of the Irishman's personality.

At 53 minutes, Celtic gained their first corner-kick, and Tully prepared to take it on the left. Characteristically, he placed the ball a few inches outside the arc at the corner flag, presumably to upset defenders. The linesman spotted the infringement and raised his flag but Tully, who probably had noticed the signal, took the kick anyway. His inswinging corner-kick deceived everybody inside the box and ended up beyond goalkeeper McFeat. Such was the overcrowding behind the goal that when the ball ended in the net, the crowd surged forward and the crush barriers gave way before them. Hundreds of spectators ended up on the pitch where, safety assured, they danced around congratulating the Celtic players and verbally abusing the Falkirk ones. The police moved quickly on to the pitch and attempted to steer the fans off the playing surface.

The linesman's flag was eventually spotted by the referee, and he moved over to the touchline to consult him; players from both sides gathered around to await the outcome. Rightly, the goal was disallowed and, for once, Charlie Tully's assiduous pursuit of 'gamesmanship' had backfired. Tully protested in vain to the referee and linesman, shrugging his shoulders in feigned helplessness and listening – hands on hips – with excessive politeness as the referee explained his decision. Tully had to take the corner-kick again but complained that he now had no room to take a run-up to the ball. Two or three policemen tried to push the crowd back onto the terracing, but Tully was still not satisfied. Almost petulantly, he handed the ball to the linesman for him to place. At last he declared himself ready and prepared to take this much-delayed corner-kick. He sent the ball on much the same flight as his previous effort; incredibly, once more it finished in the back of the net behind the luckless Archie McFeat, again untouched by any other player. The Celtic fans erupted in joy, this time mixed liberally with disbelief. They surged forward and ended up on the pitch in their thousands, and several minutes elapsed before the field could be cleared.

When the Cup tie was resumed, it had changed irrevocably in mood. Celtic, sensing this sea change, now pressed forward confidently as Falkirk understandably started to wilt. At 59 minutes, Willie Fernie crashed home the equalizer from three yards out, after two Celtic attempts at goal had been scrambled off the line by desperate defenders. Another field invasion took place but this time the supporters were on the pitch to be part of the action, and triumphalism was a convenient excuse to attempt further intimidation of the home players. Several of Falkirk's team could be seen complaining to the referee, and it was clear that the official was indicating some sympathy for their views…but the game was restarted after a lengthy delay.

Falkirk no longer had the will to resist. John McGrory, once an awkward stopper centre-half but now converted into an equally ungainly centre-forward, was chasing every ball. Cheered on by Celtic's supporters, he fastened on to a clever through pass from Fernie to smash a shot from 20 yards past McFeat. McGrory, namesake of Celtic's manager and record goalscorer, had enjoyed success in that Scottish Cup campaign with goals in the earlier rounds against lesser opposition. Inevitably, the terracing erupted and hundreds poured on to the pitch yet again, to add their unwelcome congratulations. In fact, so enthusiastic were the attentions of his admirers that McGrory had to receive treatment from Celtic's trainer.

At this point, completely and understandably exasperated by the field invasions, the referee appeared on the point of abandoning the Cup tie. As Celtic players (led by the observant Jock Stein) realised this possibility, they were quick to persuade their own supporters to leave the pitch, and ushered off the loiterers. The fact that the field invaders dispersed so promptly was the clearest indication that their presence on the playing surface had become increasingly unnecessary. After all the previous excitement, the remaining 24 minutes were played out quietly.

Charlie Tully made one other contribution to the day's entertainment: he gathered the ball near the centreline and, after beating one Falkirk defender, found his route to goal blocked. Unwilling to give up the ball, he meandered backwards towards his own goal for some 50 yards and played the ball off a Falkirk player for a Celtic goal-kick, all to the rapturous acclaim of Celtic's travelling support – a sizeable majority among the record crowd. For more than 45 minutes, Falkirk had harboured hopes of a historic first win over Celtic in the Scottish Cup, so they had a right to feel aggrieved. At the very least, the persistent fouling and attempted intimidation of Jimmy Delaney by Meechan in the first half should have brought a caution from the referee, and such an action could well have influenced the outcome of the match. Even after making allowances for the overcrowding on the terracing at the Railway End and the swaying and surging that had twisted and mangled the crush barriers, four distinct field invasions had taken place, and attempts had been made to intimidate the home players in at least three of them.

Charlie Tully's day? It was certainly eventful. Barracked by his own supporters in the first half for a lackadaisical performance, he had committed the most blatant – though scarcely brutal – foul on a genuine Celtic legend for no apparent reason, he had delighted the Celtic support with a wrong-way run towards his own goal in the closing minutes, but – most importantly of all – he had initiated the unexpected Celtic revival with a memorable (and probably unique) goal, direct from a corner-kick. And yet it could have been so much different. The referee[1] would have have been well within his rights to stop the tie, as some Celtic fans were clearly taunting the Falkirk players on the pitch and trying to intimidate them. The game would have been replayed, probably, or awarded to Falkirk – and Tully's efforts rendered irrelevant and forgotten. A later change in the rules would have meant that Tully would not have been allowed to take the corner twice, and the ball would have reverted to Falkirk for a free-kick. Consequently, Charlie Tully's moment at Brockville in February 1953 would never have occurred, and the Irishman's claim to legendary status within Celtic's pantheon would have had to rely on other exploits.

Fortunately, there have been enough instances to merit Tully's inclusion among Celtic's legendary figures. Those 90 minutes at Brockville included all the elements, positive and negative, that constituted Charlie Tully as a footballer; his career itself could have been encapsulated within that one Scottish Cup tie.

First of all, he was a remarkably talented player, possessed with skills and imagination. It takes talent, if not genius, to score from a corner-kick in the professional game, and to do it twice within a minute or so borders on the miraculous. Luck was involved, of course, and detractors – or devil's advocates – might suggest that Falkirk were not the greatest opposition in the world and that 'keeper Archie McFeat was not generally recognized as being in the top flight. Perhaps Gil Merrick of Birmingham City could sympathise with the Falkirk man, because only four months previously on 4 October 1952, while playing for England against Northern Ireland at Belfast's Windsor Park, he too was the hapless victim of another Tully corner-kick.[2]

Secondly, Charlie Tully was a character whose personality could enlighten the grimmest occasion. From his earliest days with Belfast Celtic as a teenager, he had earned the nickname of 'Cheeky Charlie'. His antics at the corner flag involving the linesman, the referee, the policemen and the encroaching supporters showed him in his normal centre-stage role, whether as comedian, martyr or hero.

Thirdly, Tully took an impish delight in practising gamesmanship or 'the art of winning without actually cheating'. Sometimes, as in the instance of the first corner-kick, he transgressed ever so slightly and this was quite deliberate on his part – a ploy designed to aggravate opposing defenders and make them lose concentration. It was not his most endearing characteristic, but it was part of his personality and had to be accepted.

Fourthly, an occasional outbreak of petulance would cause head-shaking among the more idealistic Celtic supporters. Such would be the unprovoked foul, minor as it was, on Jimmy Delaney. Pettiness of this sort was unworthy of a man wearing the green and white. Lastly, and another criticism, Tully frequently 'disappeared' physically from matches played at Cup tie pace, and this was resented by some of his teammates, most particularly Celtic's captain, Jock Stein. However, he could never be ignored and one telling contribution from Tully was enough to change the course of any match.

It will be the task of this biographer to consider Charlie Tully as a footballer, as a personality and as a human being – with all his virtues and failings. If this legend in football terms did not deserve sainthood, he certainly merits inclusion in any Celtic Hall of Fame.

## Notes

1. The match official at Brockville was Doug Gerrard (Aberdeen), a competent referee and one seldom involved in controversy; incidentally, he also refereed the Northern Ireland versus England international match in which Tully scored two goals.
2. For interest's sake, the teams for that international on 4 October 1952 were as follows:

**Northern Ireland:** Uprichard (Swindon), Cunningham (St Mirren), McMichael (Newcastle United), Blanchflower (Aston Villa), Dickson (Chelsea), McCourt (Manchester City), Bingham (Sunderland), D'Arcy (Chelsea), McMorran (Barnsley), McIlroy (Burnley), Tully (Celtic).

**England:** Merrick (Birmingham), Ramsey (Tottenham Hotspur), Eckersley (Blackburn Rovers), Wright (Wolverhampton Wanderers), Froggatt (Portsmouth), Dickinson (Portsmouth), Finney (Preston North End), Sewell (Sheffield Wednesday), Lofthouse (Bolton Wanderers), Baily (Tottenham Hotspur), Elliot (Burnley).

# Chapter 2

# *First-hand Recollections*

It would be fair, I think, to describe Malcolm Brodie, probably Northern Ireland's most distinguished sports journalist, as a Linfield sympathiser — and perhaps Rangers too — but, despite that, nobody is a greater admirer of Charlie Tully than the former sports editor and football correspondent for the *Belfast Telegraph*. 'He played with a smile on his face, an entertainer,' he tells me in Belfast. 'He may have been a Celtic icon and a true immortal of Irish football and I remember him as those, but also as an impish leprechaun of a footballer.' I knew at first hand of Charlie Tully's reputation in Glasgow and throughout Scotland, but prior to my first visit to Northern Ireland I phoned the *Belfast Telegraph* for advice. A youngish-sounding reporter at the sports desk steered me in Brodie's direction: 'Malcolm Brodie's your man. What he doesn't know about Irish football is not worth knowing. He's sort of retired nowadays but I'm sure he'll be glad to enlighten you.'

So it proves. On the phone, in answer to my initial question about Charlie Tully, his response is factual rather than boastful: 'I knew Charlie like the back of my hand' and, typical of the co-operation I was to find in Belfast, he agrees to meet me and 'talk about football'.

When we meet at Belfast's Park Avenue Hotel, I ask about the reaction in Northern Ireland to Tully's exploits at Parkhead. 'He was a Belfast boy, one of us, and the whole city rejoiced in what he achieved in Scotland. He was Northern Ireland through and through, and we all welcomed his fame and success.' He adds, taking the time to stress the point, 'You must always remember that Charlie was a star performer for a very successful Belfast Celtic side — and he was also a Northern Ireland internationalist. When people here talk about Charlie Tully and corner-kicks, they don't just mean what happened at Falkirk in the Scottish Cup.'

Within seconds, almost seamlessly, we are talking about football matches in the early 1950s. Elsewhere in the lounge of the hotel, smartly dressed young men are engrossed in sales strategies, talk of IT presentations and market projections. Everything appears modern and trendy, but we are talking about the eternal verities

Malcolm Brodie goes on to relate the famous exchange with England's Alf Ramsey at Windsor Park in the opening minutes of a Northern Ireland–England international. England had won convincingly by 6–2 and 9–2 in the two previous fixtures, but young Charles Patrick Tully was not too concerned about that; nor was he too worried that Northern Ireland had won only four times against England in the previous 70 years. In the opening seconds of the match he called out to his immediate opponent at right-back – 'Mr Ramsey, do you enjoy playing for your country?' Taken somewhat aback, the always serious Ramsey answered 'Of course, I do.' Charlie's rejoinder to that predictable answer became a classic retort throughout the province: 'In that case, make the most of this match today because after I've finished with you they'll never pick you again!' Cheek, of course, but Northern Ireland drew 2–2 with England on that 4 October 1952, and Charlie Tully scored both goals, including one direct from a corner-kick.

The day before, the *Belfast Telegraph* had already picked out Tully as the danger-man: 'Tully is the type who worries Ramsey. He can bring the ball up to him, show him it and then vanish to either side with equal ease.' Two days after the match, the same newspaper praised many performances by the home team and concluded with a note on Tully: '…wizard of the dribble and wrecker of international reputations. At last you showed your Belfast fans just how you have become the idol of Glasgow, the favourite for the wisecrack from the music hall comedian. Few greater displays have been given by any winger who ever pulled on an Irish jersey.'

It might be worth recalling the atmosphere of international matches in those days: before the match both sides had been driven out to visit Bangor Castle to be entertained jointly at a reception there, after being welcomed by the mayor. A packed Windsor Park greeted the sides when they took the pitch together, a crowd that had enjoyed two hours of pre-match entertainment.

Malcolm Brodie, a Glaswegian, remains a legend among sports writers in Northern Ireland, and he assures me that the 'conversation' with Alf Ramsey did take place. Later in our interview, he is at pains to discredit some of the other incidents attributed to Charlie Tully, and I am relieved because it adds more integrity to him as a journalist:

> Charlie was a reporter's dream; he could always be relied upon to come up with a quip or a comment that was quotable. Even better, he was more than a man who talked a good game – he produced it on the pitch more often than not. He was a bit of a stage-Irishman, but I'm going to qualify that statement in a minute. He knew very well what the world expected from an Irishman: the smile, the chuckle, the blarney, a joke or two, a pleasant manner, a jauntiness...somebody you would be glad to meet, somebody you'd want to spend time with and somebody you'd hate to leave. And that's exactly what he was (and gave). But remember this: there was nothing phoney about Charlie Tully. He was a character, a man who woke up with a smile on his face, somebody who thought every day was Christmas, to be enjoyed and savoured.

I study Brodie as he talks: a stocky man, smartly dressed in a blazer and a regimental tie, the only hint of his admitted 81 years is a lived-in face, more Scottish than Irish. His recall is impressive, the delivery is unhesitating with no lengthy pauses to remember names and places as he adds the details with pertinent observations. However, I had been worried in particular about one aspect of this biography, that – after all the facts and mass of statistics – I might not be able to 'capture' Charlie Tully as he was, 'warts and all'. I raise this anxiety: 'If I were to unearth everything about Charlie Tully, would I find things I wouldn't want to find out?' 'Well, nobody's perfect, but I don't think there was much in Charlie's life that would not bear scrutiny.' I have to be sure, and so I persist: 'Was he foul-mouthed? Or mean-spirited?' Brodie replies 'Not at all. Charlie Tully would have given you the shirt off his back; I would say he could be generous to a fault. But, before you go on in this vein, I'll tell you this. Charlie came from a respectable working-class Irish Catholic family – a large one. All his days he remained a decent Belfast boy.' I nod agreement dutifully but plough on through my prepared list of vices, both mortal and venial. 'A womaniser?' I ask. With a loud chuckle and an emphatic shake of his head, Brodie explains 'Carrie was his wife, a typical Belfast girl. She adored Charlie and he her.'

Brodie has the last word as he draws a line under this form of questioning. He speaks with the authority of a man who knows the facts and with the certainty of a lifetime in sports reporting. 'Charlie Tully was a player – and like many of his time he did not train too well – but he was a genius with a football. Most of the controversy in his life happened out there on the football pitch in front of thousands of spectators. I don't think you can ask too much more of a star player's life than that.'

Our conversation is free-flowing and far-reaching and lasts for a couple of hours but, just before leaving, I ask Brodie for a last word on Charlie Tully. 'As a man he did not have an enemy in the world; as a player he was a legend – a genuine legend,' he says. He promises to help me with any other enquiries I might have and wishes me well. On the taxi ride back into the city centre, the driver says 'Forgive me asking, but was that Malcolm Brodie you were with?' When I confirm this, he nods approvingly. 'He's your man; you can't go wrong with Malcolm Brodie.' I feel much more encouraged and ready to honour a great player whose memory has been allowed to fade into half-forgotten myths. Sometimes truth is stranger than fiction — and this could be the case with Charlie Tully.

\* \* \*

The next morning I have to meet Charlie Tully Jr, who bears a disconcerting resemblance to his famous father, despite the fact that he is 57 years old and my memory of Charlie Tully (who died at 47) is of a young man in the prime of his life. Because of the heavy traffic in the neighbourhood of Queen's University, he is a few minutes late in arriving at the guest house where I am staying, but he is full of apologies. He suggests that we go to his home for our conversation. 'It might be more relaxing over a cup of tea,' he says. I am glad of this; too often in the past, my interviews with footballers have taken place in pubs, broken up and disjointed with pauses for refreshments and interruptions from passers-by.

On the way to his house through the rush-hour traffic, he asks about the purpose of the book, and my answer is simple and truthful: to honour a great player who gave immense pleasure to spectators and supporters alike…but I feel I have to stress that it will not be a mere glorification. Facts are sacred, and often the truth is a man's best monument. 'He had his faults…' I add. His answer surprises me. 'Since you phoned, I've been thinking about things and I've reached the conclusion that I never really knew Charlie Tully. He was a stranger to me.' I am shaken by this confession, and saddened by its hint of an unhappy childhood and suggestion of neglect, perhaps good-natured but nevertheless hurtful. On a practical level, it could well mean that Charlie Tully Jr might not be able to offer too many insights or nuggets of inside information. A minute or so later, and to my considerable relief, he explains more fully. 'Charlie Tully was a public figure. He belonged to everybody in that sense – and all the world wanted to share in him. I never really knew that man.' An impression strikes me, and it is to be confirmed later, that every time he speaks of Tully as a football man – player, manager and personality – he calls him 'Charlie Tully', but at other times it is 'my father' or 'Dad'. I ask if it was hard having a famous football star as a father.

*Often it meant he was a sort of absentee figure. During the week we (my sister and I) would be at school, and that was our life. Our mother woke us up, made us breakfast, got us ready for school – and she would be waiting when we got back in the afternoon. Charlie Tully would be at Celtic Park training or away playing. Sometimes there would be a tour, or he would be out opening a store or a fête to get a few pounds above his wages – I'll come back to that later. On weekends, when most children see more of their father – Charlie Tully was working.*

I once heard – or rather overheard – Charlie Tully speak to a friend on Glasgow's Sauchiehall Street, and his son's voice is markedly similar. I tell him so, and he laughs: 'It wasn't always like that. When we came back to Belfast in 1959, I had a Scottish – well, Glasgow – accent. Reading out loud in school was torture for me. Everybody laughed at my accent.' His speaking voice is pleasant; the words are clearly enunciated, but the delivery is very quick, almost clipped at times. Similarly, his movements and gestures are brisk.

Had he inherited any of his father's skill? He claims 'As a footballer, no. Definitely not. Oh, I kicked a ball around with my dad and played with the other boys in the park and school-yard – but I never had any great ability, and I knew it.' He seems anxious to resume the topic of his father: 'Charlie Tully's talent was a God-given gift; not too many have had it.' He points out, rather unnecessarily, that his talent was recognised in a career with such clubs as Belfast Celtic, Glasgow Celtic and Northern Ireland, and this constituted fame.

Just before arriving at his house, he adds 'I'll tell you something. You must never equate fame with fortune,' and he lapses into a momentary silence as he locks his car. He nods grimly, 'Charlie Tully, when he died, was virtually penniless.' I am left to ponder this as Charlie Jr potters around his modern kitchen making the tea. I look around the spacious living room, tastefully furnished; outside, a garden is immaculately tended and a newish car sits on the driveway – all the trappings, in fact, of a comfortable middle-class life. The house itself is located in an enclave – 'Neither particularly Protestant or Catholic,' I am assured later. Charlie Jr is now semi-retired, his wife is a legal secretary and his three children are grown-up.

Somehow I had thought his children were only young. Having been told that one of his sons was at St Mary's Grammar School, I had assumed he was a pupil but, in fact, he teaches there. It is almost 60 years since Charlie Tully first played for Celtic, almost 50 years since he left Glasgow, more than 35 since he died – and now, I am told, his grandson is a teacher in a grammar school. It is another indication of the stealthy passage of time. I had picked up the latest copy of the *Celtic View* for Charlie Jr's son; interestingly, it is the issue which recalls the famous 7–1 victory over Rangers in 1957. At any rate, Charlie Jr is pleased with the gesture, assuring me that his son is the Celtic fanatic in the family and that he will devour the *Celtic View* from cover to cover.

Charlie Jr explains further when I question the 'virtually penniless' statement:

*Yes, indeed. I was only 21 when my father died, and I remember well that we had some difficulties in meeting the expenses of the funeral. To be perfectly honest, my father tended to live for the day without a thought for tomorrow; and so we rarely had any money put aside for an emergency. Remember he was only 47 when he died, and it was a bit unexpected. Only a week before, he and Carrie had been on holiday at the Beach Hotel in Mullaghmore near Sligo.*

Charlie Jr, recently engaged, was on holiday in Spain with his girlfriend when his father died so suddenly on 27 July 1971. He received a phone call at the hotel, and somebody who did not care to identify himself broke the news and asked for his comments. Charlie Jr, who had seen his father in good health just prior to leaving on his first foreign holiday, found it hard to believe. In fact, he hung up in some frustration thinking it was an ignorant joke. It was only the next day that he was contacted and informed by a member of his family.

Charlie died on a Monday night and Patricia, Tully's 17-year-old daughter, was in Galway with a group of friends. She remembers seeing a newspaper billboard telling of his death, but it simply did not register with her until the police called at the guest house to break the news to her. She left for Belfast right away, travelling by bus, and arrived home about midnight.

Brian, the youngest of Tully's children at 10 years of age, was in bed and slept through his father's death but was wakened by the commotion and taken to a neighbour's house, where he spent the night. Carrie had to break the news to him the next morning at the breakfast table. 'I have something awful sad to tell you...' and according to Patricia, 'he dropped his wee head on to the table, beside the corn flakes.'

'Virtually penniless' hardly fits the description of a family that can afford and enjoy holidays, I think to myself: Charlie and Carrie at Mullaghmore, Charlie Jr in Spain and Patricia in Galway. As Charlie Jr says though, his father lived for the day; the holidays suggest a happy, well-adjusted family enjoying some of life's simple pleasures. Charlie Jr goes on to describe the funeral:

*One good thing about the shock of my father dying so young was that I realised the importance of planning ahead for a rainy day, so to speak. And I've been a careful man with money. It must be almost unbelievable for you to find out that Charlie Tully could not pay for his own funeral...I remember that Celtic were well represented at the occasion: the manager Jock Stein — who played alongside my father — was there, as was Sean Fallon, who sponsored me for my First Communion; the goalkeeper John Bonnar and director Jim Farrell were also there; Billy McNeill, Celtic's captain, was there — all of them acted as pall-bearers up the Falls Road to Milltown Cemetery. That was a local tradition; the coffin would be carried along the Falls Road to the cemetery, and traffic would be held up if there was a big turn-out such as for my father. I was told later that the club wanted to send an even bigger delegation but the police (and the army) advised very much against it. This was at the height of 'The Troubles', remember. I will always remember the kindness shown to me by Billy McNeill on the day of the funeral. He came over to express his sympathy to my mother and other members of the family, and later on he sought me out to have a private word: 'Charlie, I know this must have come as a great shock but, as the man of the house now, you'll have to make some important decisions. If things are rough in any way, I want you to ring me and let me know; if you need anything — even just to talk about things — ring me.' I was very touched by that gesture, and before he left to go back to Glasgow he reminded me: 'Don't hesitate to ask for any help, financial or anything else. Remember Celtic owe Charlie Tully more than they can ever repay.'*

Charlie Tully Jr goes on to say with some pride 'We never did pick up the phone to ask for financial help. In the end, we managed. Afterwards my mother put Charlie Tully's memorabilia up for auction – caps, medals, jerseys – I think she got £3,000 for the lot and, as far as I knew, she put it aside and never spent it. She was very different from my dad that way.' Billy McNeill bears out the story:

> *Charlie's funeral was unbelievable. Crowds lined the street all the way to the cemetery a couple of miles away, and thousands more were at the cemetery itself. I had never seen anything like it. To be perfectly honest, I wasn't aware of his straitened circumstances. An awful pity that. If he had played at a later time, he would have retired with thousands. I can tell you, though, that young Charlie never got in touch to ask for help – and that says a lot for him and his family.*

John Bonnar was also one of the pall-bearers. Astonished at the number of people – ordinary men, women and children – who lined the Falls Road to the cemetery, he turned to say to Jock Stein 'Look at those crowds! Charlie would have loved this.'

Charlie Jr remembers:

> *It was a hard time for us. My grandmother (Carrie's widowed mother) lived with her sister at 9 St James Road, and all of us from Glasgow spent our summer holidays there. After my father left Celtic, we returned to Belfast and had to move in there with them. A small terraced house off the Falls Road, very crowded, but we were still living there when Charlie died in 1971 – an indication of how financially strapped we were. Hard to believe these days.*

Charlie Jr suggests that life in such a district was not easy. In Glasgow, the Tully family sometimes went to Mass in the Gorbals – and this was before Sir Basil Spence's experiment in social engineering. Charlie Jr remembers the depressing sight of street after street of soot-begrimed tenements. His father used to visit a friend, David Hope (incidentally a keen Rangers' supporter), in Dennistoun, another deprived area at that time. 'I used to play round the back, kicking a ball against a wash-house wall while the visit was going on. I used to look around, looking up at the tenements, all grey and grimy.' He also recalls his mother telling him that his father often did not have enough cash to pay for the tram ride to Celtic Park from the city centre – and it would only be a few pennies in those days. But Audrey Douglas, long-time secretary to Jimmy McGrory at Celtic Park and who married Willie Fernie, shakes her head at that particular recollection: 'If Charlie was short of his fare, it was his own fault. I used to give the players extra money in addition to their wages for such expenses. That Charlie, a terrible man with money he was.' Audrey and her husband lived near Charlie and Carrie in Clarkston. She remembers Willie and Charlie getting the bus into the city centre and the tram to the East End from the stop just outside the Argyll Arcade between Buchanan Street and Queen Street. The bus? The tram? It is a sharp reminder that few players in those days could think of buying and running a car. Occasionally Charlie would raise the matter of money with Desmond White, the secretary, who would remind him he was already getting the best wages possible.

I ask about Tully's death and if it was very unexpected. Charlie Jr replies:

*I remember he used to go round for pick-up games at the old Celtic Park here in Belfast. Even when he was out of shape he could occasionally produce a brilliant move, including his famed scissor-kick. Once, the other players applauded but they insisted it was a fluke, that he could never repeat it. That just made my father all the more determined, and before the end of the session he had scored a goal with yet another scissor-kick. I've been told, though, that often he would have to take a rest in those games, being out of breath. One of the happiest memories I have is of Sunday afternoons after Mass. We would go along to Celtic Park, closed down and locked up by then, but we were always allowed in. Charlie Tully's name could open doors all over Belfast. I was there, Charlie Tully was there, three boys named O'Reilly who lived across St John's Road from us, usually a couple of Irish League players – and anybody else who came along for the kick-around. It was mainly five-a-sides and highly informal, with no real hard physical tackling. Charlie was at his happiest, in his element, playing football on the beautiful turf of Celtic Park, still lovingly tended and manicured – and inside the ghost of a stadium. I think lots of memories flitted across his mind: playing for Celtic against Linfield, hearing the roar of the crowd… The memories must have flooded back. Charlie Tully just loved playing football, from childhood on; he never lost that enthusiasm for it, never. Like an Irish Walter Mitty, I too could imagine playing for Belfast Celtic (as my father had done) before those crowds of fanatical supporters. What would Charlie Tully have been thinking? He never said, but he was enjoying himself out there at 40 years of age, admittedly a bit heavier than in his playing days but still with all his old tricks. Dad would get the ball and come towards you with a smile on his face, and he could always get by you almost effortlessly. One of the younger players, after trying for ages to get the ball off him, told me – and he was panting by then – 'Sure, it's always a pleasure to be nutmegged by Charlie Tully!'. I remember one trick he had: he'd have the ball and would slow down as he approached you. And then he would raise his left arm quite slowly and point out to the wing. You knew fine he was not going that way and the ball wasn't either, but you fell for it every time. He would stretch that arm out and pretend to be looking at his watch to tell the time, and even then you couldn't get the ball off him. Sometimes it was like the Harlem Globetrotters out there on Celtic Park.*

Charlie Tully Jr, after talking about his father's death, offers me another cup of tea and, when I decline with thanks, wonders if I would like to see some memorabilia that he has retained. Together, we pore over a treasure trove of family photographs and clippings. Surprisingly, Charlie does not recognise some Celtic players in the photographs and, when I identify them for him, his interest appears a bit feigned. He seems to have moved on from being the son of a famous footballer and carved out a life of his own. I had asked him about the difficulties of growing up as the son of Charlie Tully. Bringing the question up to date, I ask if it is still hard being the son of a star.

*I'm my father's son all right; like him, I'm a bit impulsive but — and this might come as a surprise for you — Charlie Tully was often shy. He could put on an act and be very sociable. I think I'm retiring too, but I don't have the need to put on a bit of a show like my father. People expected different things from him. His children — myself, Patricia and Brian — knew he was a great player and made news all the time, but we never quite realised just what a player he must have been. Bertie Peacock was a friend of my father's from the 1950s on and always kept in touch with me. When Jock Stein died in 1985, he phoned me up and asked me to travel to Glasgow for the funeral. I was a bit reluctant — shy, I suppose — but Bertie insisted. He told me that he and I would be representing my father there. I was taken under Bertie's wing and went to several functions;*

*Bertie introduced me to various celebrities in the world of British football. I particularly remember Alex Ferguson; when we were introduced, he said 'Charlie Tully's son? What a player he was!'*

Charlie Jr hesitates before he continues:

*I feel a bit guilty because I don't really know enough about my father as a player — and it's too late now for that. As you can see, his autobiography [Passed to You] is there in front of you, but it's very skimpy, I feel. I've never cashed in on his fame and rarely draw attention to it, but since his death I've learned a bit more about him as a footballer and a personality — I suppose he would be considered a celebrity nowadays. When I have more time, I'm thinking of trying to get a website together to do him justice as well. I think he deserves a memorial like that.*

# Chapter 3

## *Baptism(s)*

Charlie Tully was in excellent company when he made his international debut for Northern Ireland[1] against England on 9 October 1948. He was in no doubt that his transfer to Celtic and his sparkling form for the Glasgow club had made it easier for him to be recognised, as the Irish selectors appeared to favour players who had made their mark on the mainland. The teams lined up as follows:

**Northern Ireland:** Smyth (Wolverhampton), Carey (Manchester United), Martin (Aston Villa), W. Walsh (Manchester City), Vernon (West Bromwich Albion), Farrell (Everton), O'Driscoll (Swansea), McAlinden (Southend United), D. Walsh (West Bromwich Albion), Tully (Celtic), Eglinton (Everton).

**England:** Swift (Manchester City), Scott (Arsenal), Howe (Derby County), Wright (Wolverhampton), Franklin (Stoke City), Cockburn (Manchester United), Matthews (Blackpool), Mortensen (Blackpool), Milburn (Newcastle United), Pearson (Manchester United), Finney (Preston North End).

Northern Ireland, urged on by a fervent Windsor Park crowd, pressed from the start and threatened to outplay the favoured England, but the visitors weathered the early storm. England's first goal was a personal disaster for Irish goalkeeper Smyth; he made little effort to deal with a cross from Stanley Matthews, judging that the ball was going past, but the ball swerved late in flight and ended up in the net. Tully had been prominent early in the Irish attacks, and Billy Wright, at the height of his powers, had to deal carefully with him. Shortly after Matthews's goal, Tully missed a glorious chance to equalise. Cheekily, he prodded the ball from Frank Swift's hand as he prepared to clear, and rounded the giant English goalkeeper. In Tully's own words, 'He [Swift] pushed me and, when I tried to connect, the ball hit my toes and went high over the bar. Willie Webb, the well-known Scottish referee, says to this day that if I had fallen he'd have given a penalty. But he had given me the advantage rule and I hadn't taken it.' Overall class told in the end, and England ran out comfortable 6–2 winners, with other goals coming from Mortensen (three), Milburn and Pearson.

\* \* \*

Charlie Tully had made his eagerly awaited debut for Celtic two months earlier. He had played reasonably well in the club's pre-season trial matches, and word was filtering out of Celtic Park that the young Irishman (a veteran at the age of 24) was indeed a special player, based on the impressions he had made while training. On 14 August 1948, a Saturday, the first Olympic Games after World War Two were drawing to an end in London, marked by the nostalgic strains of the *Londonderry Air*, perhaps better known as *Danny Boy*; the Fifth Test was in its second day at the Oval, with the all-conquering Australians bowling England out for 52 runs (out of which Len Hutton made 30) then making 287 for 5 (despite the great Don Bradman being bowled for a duck in his last Test match). But football was the order of the day in Scotland, and the biggest crowd was at Celtic Park to see Charlie Tully make his debut.

He could not have had a more testing baptism, as Morton, defeated Scottish Cup finalists after a replay with Rangers in April, had one of the best defences in the League. In fact, Morton were slight favourites to beat Celtic even at Celtic Park; it was anticipated that Celtic would miss their regular pivot Willie Corbett (recently transferred to Preston

North End), whose place would be taken by the relatively unknown Alec Boden. Although they had also flirted with relegation in the previous campaign, Morton were formidable and fielded five ex-Queen's Park players against Celtic. It was yet another indication of the ambition of the Greenock club, who had also enticed several English internationals to turn out for them during the wartime seasons. The line up was as follows:

**Celtic:** Miller, Milne, Mallan, Evans, Boden, McAuley, Weir, McPhail, Lavery, Tully, Paton.

**Morton:** Cowan, Mitchell, Whigham, Campbell, Miller, Whyte, Hepburn, Murphy, Farquhar, Orr, Mochan.

The match was played in brilliant sunshine before a crowd estimated at just over 55,000 – a remarkable turnout to watch a team that had performed so poorly throughout the latter half of the previous season. Morton had beaten Celtic 1–0 after extra-time in the Scottish Cup semi-final at Ibrox on 27 March and had thrashed Celtic 4–0 in their last League encounter at Cappielow, so they were rightly confident and introduced a debutant of their own at outside-left, Neil Mochan. Tully was at inside-left and marked by Billy Campbell, a highly rated right-half permanently on the fringe of international honours but often overlooked in favour of Anglo Scots. One of the features of the match was the confidence shown by the Morton defenders in their international 'keeper Jimmy Cowan; Campbell, in particular, had few qualms about firing the ball back to him from 30 yards out.

Tully had only one particular moment of brilliance in the second half, when he shuffled in from the wing and half-curled, half-hooked a shot from the edge of the penalty area that had Cowan scrambling across his goal, helpless as the ball scraped the far junction of the post and crossbar. It was Celtic's best attempt at goal as the forwards struggled to break free of a well-organised defence. The effort was greeted with a round of applause, as if to encourage a player who appeared already to be a cut above his colleagues in football intelligence. American sports-writers have a phrase for such results as a 0–0 draw – 'like kissing your own sister' – and there was a tinge of letdown in the air. On the whole, Celtic disappointed. One newspaper *(Evening Citizen)* commented 'There was no indication that Celtic had anything beyond last season's zeal streaked with desperation.' Elsewhere, the contest was described as 'cup-tie football with dour tackles and determined chases which gave neither team much scope for finesse'.

The only thing that raised spirits was that Rangers had drawn at Motherwell (1–1), and their centre-half Willie Woodburn had been ordered off. Surprisingly, in view of his quiet debut, the headline in the next day's *Sunday Mail* read 'THIS BOY TULLY WILL BRING MUCH JOY TO CELTIC!'

\* \* \*

A bit more than six years previously (in 1942), Charlie Tully – only 17 at the time – had made a surprise debut for Belfast Celtic. At least it was a complete shock for young Tully, who had been told to report to Celtic Park for a friendly against a Glentoran Select. But 30 minutes before the kick-off, Elisha Scott – the legendary manager of Belfast Celtic – sought out Tully, who had seated himself in the stand with his friends, to tell him he was playing. Although he had originally been associated with Celtic as a net boy and as a young prospect, Tully was astounded at the promotion. According to Tully in his autobiography, he was 'for once in my life speechless'. It might be surprising to relate but the youngster was so overawed that he had to be helped into his strip – the green-and-white hoops similar to Glasgow Celtic's:

*I was so astounded, shaky and embarrassed that when I got to the dressing-room among such greats as Tommy Breen, Bertie Fulton, Jack Vernon, Jimmy McAlinden and Syd McIlroy, I had to be literally dressed for battle. Jack Vernon pulled the green and white jersey over my head, and Jimmy McAlinden pushed my first pair of shin guards down my stockings. Before this I had used magazines and newspapers.*
(*Passed to You*, Stanley Paul, 1958)

Belfast Celtic lost that match 3–1, but the youngster impressed Scott enough for the manager to offer him terms. According to Tully – admittedly not the most reliable witness – 'the newspapers proclaimed next day that the boy Tully was the only find of the game. He did more than any of the established stars. This schoolboy is an outstanding discovery for the future'.

And so began an often stormy relationship with Elisha Scott. In an attempt to curb the youngster, Scott once handed him a bucket of whitewash and a paintbrush, telling him to paint the goalposts and crossbars at each end of Celtic Park. Charlie was not too pleased and carried out the task without much enthusiasm. He reported back to Elisha Scott's tiny office after an hour, and the manager went out to inspect his handiwork. 'Not bad, son, but they need another coat. So, get to work.' The promising star was livid by then: 'What am I supposed to learn from this?' Scott took him by the shoulder and on to the pitch: 'I want you to have those goals gleaming white – so that on Saturdays you might just remember that the ball is supposed to go between them every now and then.'

It was the custom for youthful signings, or apprentices, to be given menial tasks such as cleaning the boots of the senior players, marking the lines on the pitch or tidying up the dressing room after training. Such actions were intended to make the newcomer more familiar with his surroundings and also establish or reinforce a pecking order within the playing staff. Once the youngster had shown his readiness to conform – and had revealed talent in training or in reserve games – he was promoted to the occasional appearance for the club's first XI. Then, if he did well, he would be fully accepted by the other players, with the possible exception of the man he had displaced. Elisha Scott, a famous goalkeeper with Liverpool and an Irish international, recognised that his new player was a special case and one to be handled carefully.

Elisha Scott, a non-Catholic, was manager of Belfast Celtic from 1934 onwards and was an astonishing character. He refused to have a telephone in his home, considering it an intrusion on his family life, and has been described as a Bill Shankly type of manager, ruling his club with an iron fist. Upon his transfer from Liverpool to Belfast Celtic, he had been diagnosed with a congenital heart problem but chose to ignore it and played for a further two seasons as Belfast Celtic's goalkeeper, gaining the last three of his 31 caps for Northern Ireland. Goalkeepers are often considered eccentric, but Elisha Scott stood out; on the football pitch he always wore three sweaters, even in a heatwave, and favoured tights (long johns dyed black with stitched-on knee pads) in cold weather. In his autobiography, Tully relates that Mr Scott handed him a book of rules. For today's players some of these rules have a curiously old-fashioned ring: 'You are a Belfast Celtic player now; no matter who you are, first or second team man, be at the ground at the times scheduled; if you can't read this, I'll read it out to you; if you are ill, phone the club doctor or trainer; if the club travels by train or bus, be at the meeting place thirty minutes beforehand; and remember, there's only one skipper on the park.'

Recognising the impish side of Tully's nature, the manager had to exert a lot of discipline on the young star, who did not relish the rigours of fitness training nor the chores expected of him. At Celtic Park he had to carry away the cut grass regularly, brush out the stands after the greyhound meetings and wash the baths – tasks that the youthful Charlie probably resented, pointing out that he was an apprentice footballer and not an apprentice odd-job man. Confrontations with Elisha Scott were frequent but the manager remained firm, even after the player became a regular in Belfast Celtic's side. His threat remained, 'Remember I'm the boss until you're elected to take my place. Otherwise, you'll be back painting goalposts and lighting boilers.'

## Note

1. For the sake of clarity I have consistently called this international side 'Northern Ireland', although for many years they called themselves 'Ireland'. I have similarly designated the Republic of Ireland side as 'Eire', as I believe this was the more common appellation during Charlie Tully's career.

# Chapter 4
## *Life Before Glasgow*

Among the memorabilia Charlie Tully Jr showed me was an independent magazine devoted to Belfast social history called *Rushlight*. I was intrigued by the unselfconscious glimpses it gave of life in the old Falls Road, and Charlie allowed me to take it away along with family photographs. When I studied it later in the guest house, I was taken by its descriptions of events, places and customs about the time when Charlie Tully was growing up. According to the magazine, 'The streets [near the Falls Road] were commonly lighted by gas till the 1950s, and in some old shops customers could buy cooked pigs' feet, and stew by the bowl – while water was delivered in buckets by carters from a well near Divis Street.'

The magazine waxed more lyrical about 'the Phoenix Bar with a pot-bellied stove. Some of the greatest characters in Belfast gathered round that old fire; there would be winos, wheelers, dealers, spoofers, and maybe a doctor or teacher who had walked away from their professions for the life of drink and craic'. Among the customers were 'Jimmy "Blue-Bum", the meths drinker; "Corky", a big woman who'd lash out at any man near her, and Paddy "the Rebel", who could recite the 1916 Proclamation at the drop of a hat. Paddy "Hard Times" could tell a sorrowful story, Paddy "Dirt" played the spoons and "Doctor" McNab delighted picture house queues with his singing.'

Malcolm Brodie had described Charlie Tully's background to me as 'a respectable Catholic family', and indeed it was. Charlie's father (also named Charles) served in the British Army in two World Wars: in the Great War (1914–18), he lied about his age to enlist and serve with the Royal Ulster Rifles, and he enrolled with the Royal Artillery in World War Two (1939–45), despite his age. His mother (Mary Anne) – with 12 children to raise – was a stay-at-home mother, as was the custom in those days. After serving in World War One, Charles did work at the (predominantly Protestant) Harland & Wolff shipyard but, unhappy there mainly because of shop-floor discrimination, he lasted only a year before taking up permanent employment with the Belfast Corporation's Cleansing Department. They were, as said, a respectable family, and life was hard at 174 McDonnell Street. Charles was in regular, full employment but wages were low, and Mary Anne, a small wiry woman, worked just as hard at home.

Charles Patrick Tully was born at home in McDonnell Street, just off the Falls Road in North Belfast, on 11 July 1924. He was the second child born to Charles and Mary Tully. Typically, Charlie made much of the fact that he was born close to 12 July, claiming that the noise and celebration from a certain neighbouring district was in honour of his birth. Some weeks later, he was baptised at St John's – where he would be married and buried.

Like so many in the 1920s and 1930s, the family frequently struggled to get by. Present-day children born into such circumstances often drift into trouble and petty crime. Not so with young Charlie. A football-mad boy aware of his talent from an early age, he would travel miles to find a game. It did not matter where or with whom; he wanted to play football, and little else mattered. He was too busy kicking a ball (on the street, in vacant lots or in public parks) to get into any trouble.

In Belfast, in those days, football was sometimes categorised as a British game, while hurling would have been the preferred sport of many Republicans or Nationalists in the Falls Road. It was strictly 'no-contest' for Charles Patrick Tully – and this meant that he came into frequent contact with Protestant boys. Everybody I consulted about Charlie Tully insists that he was totally free of any hang-ups arising from religion and politics in Belfast. Perhaps some of that arose from his clear preference for football over any other sport, which allowed him to mix with the opposite side of the religious divide that characterised Belfast.

To his dying day Charlie Tully was obsessed with football. Accordingly, he appeared fated to end up in Glasgow, a hotbed of the game. At Celtic Park, where players of different faiths played for the club, there would be little or no problems arising out of religion. Occasionally, disputes and quarrels would arise, but these were mainly due to specific grievances or the squabbles to be expected among high-spirited and energetic young men. The much-reported fist-fight between Bobby Evans and Charlie Tully in 1957 arose out of a disagreement and was heightened by two distinct personality types. Religion had nothing to do with it.

Charlie's autobiography *Passed to You* is of little help in depicting clearly the hardships undoubtedly endured in his childhood. A couple of sentences dismiss the neighbourhood and early years: 'Mine were hard, but carefree, and are still the happiest of my life. They were barefoot days. Times that will never be recaptured no matter how much money or how much glory comes my way in the future. Money was of no account – for there was never any money to count. Pleasures were simple. What's for dinner? When are the school holidays? And where's our next game of football coming from?'

In conversation with me, his brother Billy – who still lives in the neighbourhood – described the Falls Road in the 1930s as 'a typical working-class district with a pub on every corner and lots of bookies', but that hardly does justice to this area even today. First of all, it was virtually an all-Catholic ghetto and for a long time that meant 'impoverished' in Belfast terms, with overcrowded terrace houses, massive unemployment among the heads of families and little prospect of improvement. *Rushlight*, while commemorating the past in such districts as the Falls Road, makes little effort to glorify or glamorise those hard times. Elsewhere, it has become a romantic cliché to consider that life in such districts in Belfast and the Gorbals in Glasgow was somehow ennobling…but the reality was vastly different.

An article on nicknames caught my eye, and it might be interesting to speculate on the origin of those such as Paddy 'Hard Times', 'Spud' Murphy, 'Gas Meter' Peter Marky,

'Girnin' Tommy, 'Hitler' Foster, 'Snooker' McDade and 'Red' Dan, as well as Jimmy 'Blue Bum' and the others previously mentioned. Similarly, an article about St Kevin's School – which both Charlie Tully (in the 1930s) and his son (in the 1960s) attended – was revealing. The school opened in 1933, and its first headmaster was the highly respected Gaelic scholar and later trade unionist John Duffin. Charlie Tully, according to his son, remembered Mr Duffin, but did he know that two of the headmaster's brothers had been murdered in a sectarian action by members of the RIC (Royal Irish Constabulary, the forerunner of the RUC) at 64 Clonard Gardens in April 1921? According to *Rushlight*, 'John had laid his two dead brothers side by side on the kitchen floor before he had awakened his father and two younger brothers who had heard nothing.' Of some interest in the magazine is a photograph (circa 1935 or 1936) of St Kevin's Under-14 team, in which a very young Charlie Tully is featured. There are 15 boys in the photograph, all kitted out, along with two teachers and the parish priest. It may not have been a soccer team though, as the school was more encouraging of Gaelic sports, especially hurling.

Charlie had become a pupil at St Kevin's after a couple of years at Slate Street School, another Catholic Primary School, near his home in the Lower Falls Road. As previously mentioned, Charlie's childhood was one of real deprivation, apart from the comforts gleaned from a large and close-knit family. Charlie Tully Jr reconstructs it thus:

*McDonnell Street was razed to the ground later or, in the words of the tenants, 'condemned' as sub-standard. When you consider what was allowed to remain, it must have been awful (by today's standards). I seem to remember little snippets from my father and uncles: a small terraced house, a cobbled street lit by gas lamps – and an outside toilet. And remember this was a large family. Even in 1924 (when Charlie was born) McDonnell Street was considered old.*

In its depiction of slum life in Cork, the best-selling novel *Angela's Ashes* utilised wit and humour, and charm and absurdity to show these conditions as a backdrop for comedy. However, in real life the grinding poverty, constant squalor and permanent deprivation is the setting for tragedy. The most common philosophy becomes an inarticulate stoicism; poor people simply get on with it with no time for resentment, as everybody is in the same boat. How could you get out of such surroundings? Children left school at the earliest possible age, usually 14, and then looked for work. The more fortunate were taken on as apprentices in one of the trades; the less lucky became labourers, while they waited to become cannon-fodder in World Wars.

Luck or talent was the route. Often the talent was in such popular sports as boxing or football, and it is significant that in such deprived countries as Scotland and Northern Ireland, the best boxers have been little men – a possible indication of general malnutrition. More opportunities existed in football, but talent was not the only factor. A player needed luck to be spotted by a scout for senior teams and to survive in the harsh world of semi-professional football, injury-free. Those seeking a career in football were slow to realise (or perhaps they chose to ignore the odds) that the path from Govan tenement to Cheshire mansion (or from log-cabin to White House) is an unlikely one. Sir Alex Ferguson (and Abraham Lincoln) are the exceptions rather than the rule.

Sean Fallon, a fellow Irishman, recognises some of the difficulties his friend and teammate faced: 'Charlie came from the Falls Road, a tough part of the world, and he knew a lot of what was going on but he never got himself involved in anything. He enjoyed life – and trouble was the last thing he would want.' Sean, of course, came from Sligo – a contrast from the Falls Road area – where his father was highly respected and, indeed, its mayor for a period.

Because of the ban on football at school, Charlie went wandering around the city to find games of football. When he did get a chance, he was always invited back; a boy who could dribble like this tiny tot was a find indeed. Genuine talent has a habit of overcoming any possible prejudice, and the youngster got a game or two for a predominantly Protestant side whose coach quickly discovered the religion of the newcomer. This man took the trouble to arrange for the boy to meet another teacher at a Catholic school, where he started to play regularly, and he was recommended for a job as a net boy at Celtic Park. Inevitably, the youngster was invited to play a trial match for Belfast Celtic, and the rest is history.

Just when his performances for Belfast Celtic were attracting attention from prominent clubs in mainland Britain, including Arsenal, Wolverhampton Wanderers, Sunderland and Liverpool, he was taken ill and hospitalised for three weeks. Billy Tully claims that Manchester United were particularly interested in signing him; but after a scout visited him in hospital, following a severe bout of glandular fever in his mid-teens, the English club felt that the youngster, weak and under-nourished after the illness, would never be strong enough to make it as a professional.

For a while, interest in the promising Irish player waned but was renewed later, with Glasgow Celtic exhibiting a keen awareness of the developing situation. Tully, now a regular at Belfast Celtic as an inside-forward, was maturing as a player. Frequently, Charlie suffered from a rash on his neck that tended to flare up in hot weather. Long before Eric Cantona, Charlie Tully played with the collar up on his jersey, either for comfort or perhaps vanity.

Celtic's decline in the world of Scottish football was clearly revealed in a short tour of Ireland in April 1947. The team party consisted of the following: Willie Miller, Rolando Ugolini, Bobby Hogg, Jimmy Mallan, Roy Milne, John McPhail, Willie Corbett, Robert Quinn, Frank Quinn, Gerry McAloon, Tommy Kiernan, Joe Rae, Bobby Evans, Willie

Gallacher and Tommy Bogan. At the time, not too many of that squad would have been considered for inclusion in a Celtic Hall of Fame. On 15 April 1947 they drew 4–4 with Belfast Celtic in the first match between the two clubs since 1936. The team line ups were as follows:

**Belfast Celtic:** Sloan, McMillan, Simpson, Lawler, Ferguson, Wilson, Campbell, McGarry, Jones, Tully, Bonnar.

**Glasgow Celtic:** Miller, Hogg, Mallan, McPhail, Corbett, Milne, Quinn, McAloon, Kiernan, Evans, Bogan.

Early on, the Parkhead men led by 2–1 but trailed by 3–2 before half-time, with three goals coming from the bustling centre-forward Jimmy Jones – destined to be a famous figure in Belfast football history. Celtic needed two late goals to scramble an unconvincing draw – a result that surprised many in Belfast who had been raised on tales of Glasgow Celtic's invincibility. Malcolm Brodie was more charitable: 'I rather think the Glasgow men approached it more like a training session; they stirred themselves when they were 4–2 down near the end.'

Two days later, the Celtic party travelled westwards and played Derry City before a record crowd at Brandywell. It was another disappointing result for the tourists. The home side, although struggling in last place in their own league, played well and scored the winner three minutes from the end to eke out a 1–0 win. On the same day, back at Hampden Park, the Scottish Cup Final between Aberdeen and Hibernian took place. Almost needless to say, these were two of the clubs who had made genuine efforts to provide meaningful football during the war, unlike Celtic.

The last fixture was on 21 April, and Celtic improved with a 3–0 win over Shamrock Rovers, but the game had to be abandoned with 20 minutes left because of torrential rain. It was a forgettable tour by an undistinguished side, but the Celtic management team had seen enough of Charlie Tully to start considering making an approach for him.

A year later a Celtic bid for Tully was accepted (while the Glasgow club's inside-forward Gerry McAloon – who scored two goals in Belfast – moved in the opposite direction a few weeks later). *The Irish News* speculated 'As there is no maximum wage in Scottish football, Charlie should be on big money if he can command a place in the league team.' At that time, footballers in Northern Ireland earned only about £4 a week. Belfast Celtic players would receive occasional bonuses, usually for matches against local rivals Linfield and Glentoran.

Belfast Celtic, meanwhile, had continued their domination of football in Northern Ireland. On 19 April 1947 they sealed the final Regional League title with a 2–1 win over Cliftonville at home, with Charlie Tully and Jimmy Jones scoring the goals. A week or so later, young Tully scored again, this time getting the only goal in the Irish Cup Final between Belfast Celtic and Glentoran. Taking full advantage of momentary indecision between two defenders, Charlie Tully picked up the loose ball and raced through the open space to drive a left-foot shot past the 'keeper, McKee. For that important match, Elisha Scott had picked Eddie McMorran and dropped Jimmy Jones, who had scored three times against Celtic and had finished top scorer for Belfast Celtic. It was yet another indication that Mr Scott was very much the man in charge at Celtic Park – and probably another reminder to Tully that nobody was indispensable. Elisha Scott was like a father to young Charlie as a footballer, and Tully came to recognise this belatedly.

In June 1948 Celtic's chairman Bob Kelly and manager Jimmy McGrory travelled to Belfast with a cheque for around £8,000, ready to discuss terms with Charlie Tully. With unconscious irony, the player wrote in his autobiography 'I had a lot of time to think things over. I knew I would be sorry to leave my family, friends, and pals, but on the other hand there was the future to think of — something I hadn't done much of before. I was coming up for twenty-two years of age.[1] I was engaged to my childhood sweetheart, Carrie Harris, and when I told this to Jimmy McGrory, he'd promised me a house, an important detail which clinched matters for me.' Two weeks later, he travelled across the Irish Sea to Glasgow on the *Royal Ulsterman* to start pre-season training.

\* \* \*

When I visited Belfast in October 2007 to interview people for this book, Celtic were playing Benfica in Lisbon in the Champions League, and I was keen to watch the match in a pub on the Falls Road. It was a mistake.

On a bus tour that afternoon, the district had looked lively in the sunlight — vibrant and bustling — and the tour guide was optimistic that the process of gentrification would transform it further. At dusk, with night approaching, it appeared more threatening, and the only activity was the occasional firecracker let off by some youngsters in a rehearsal for Hallowe'en a few days later. The explosions were disconcerting, a reminder of more damaging ones in the past. Discarded newspapers swirled in the wind, littering the occasional vacant space where a building had been razed. The pub — guaranteed by the taxi-driver to show the Celtic match — was just as gloomy inside as out. The linoleum on the floor was stained with beer, phlegm, tobacco and anything else imaginable. A dozen people, nobody younger than 40, were dotted around the dingy bar. It resembled a TV commercial for depression. A silence broke out at my entrance; apparently strangers are still viewed with a degree of suspicion in these parts. I nodded to a couple of the customers and, noting the bartender was busy pulling a Guinness, I studied the Celtic memorabilia on display around the walls: Jock Stein's contract, an Old Firm programme from the 1960s and the inevitable team photograph of the Lisbon Lions.

When I turned round, everybody was staring at me, pints forgotten in the spectacle of a stranger in the Falls Road. 'Some team, that one,' I started, pointing to the Lions. 'You're a Celtic man, then?' a spokesman for the assembly asked, with more than a touch of hostility in his voice. 'Sure, isn't everybody?' My attempt at humour fell flat. 'In that case, you'll have no trouble naming the European Cup team for us,' came an invitation delivered with a menacing rasp. It was definitely a test, but what would be the consequences of any memory-lapse on my part? Did they still do knee-capping here? 'Simpson, Craig, Gemmell, Murdoch, McNeill, Clark, Johnstone…' I had passed that test, but I was still far from comfortable. I looked over at a coven of women, who looked old enough to be grandmothers, in the corner. Exchanging recipes for spells and incantations over their bottles of Sweetheart Stout, they gave the distinct impression of being a permanent fixture, perhaps even since the 1960s, I thought unkindly, noting clapped-in cheeks and heavily veined hands. How was I going to get out of here gracefully?…'Do you serve pub grub?' I asked the man behind the bar, now free to serve me. As I hoped, the pub did not serve food; and strangely, nobody among the locals could recall a pub (in a street with one on every corner) that actually served food. A chippie might be my best bet, it was suggested by one denizen, and I agreed, assuring the informant that I would be back in time for the match. I lied. There was no way I would be returning to that drab hostelry, at least not without a generous supply of anti-depressants.

I stood conspicuous at a deserted street corner for 10 anxious minutes before I could stop a taxi and head into the more upmarket city centre. Safe in the taxi, I looked again at the receding surroundings. If this was improvement — and there were clear indications it was — what on earth was it like back in 1924 when Charlie Tully was born and lived in 174 McDonnell Street, now long gone?

## Note
1. Charlie appears to be arithmetically challenged here. If he was born on 11 July 1924, he must have been 23 years of age in May 1948.

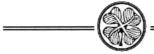

# Chapter 5

# *Sudden Impact*

When Charlie Tully came to Glasgow in 1948, he was not the only new capture Celtic had made in their attempts to arrest the slide towards mediocrity or worse. The other man was 65-year-old Jimmy Hogan, revered throughout Europe as a coach but largely ignored in Britain. His age would prove to be his biggest drawback in gaining total acceptance at Celtic Park; Scottish players were notoriously negative in their attitude to coaching with Jimmy Hogan, describing his initial reaction 'as if each and every one was saying "What can this old codger show us?"'

When Hungary shocked the football world by humiliating England 6–3 at Wembley (and later by 7–1 in Budapest), coach-manager Gustav Sebes proclaimed 'We played football as Jimmy Hogan taught us. When our soccer history is told, his name should be written in gold letters.' And yet, when this fit and spry man was employed at Celtic Park, several of the more established players – the same ones who had dragged Celtic down into the relegation quagmire the previous season – failed to listen, with two notable exceptions being Tommy Docherty and Johnny Paton, who were the only two to have a lengthy career in football after their playing days were over. Tommy Docherty spent only one year at Celtic Park but recognised his debt to Jimmy Hogan: 'I took to him very quickly, and so did several of the other young players at Celtic Park at the time. Some of the established stars would have nothing to do with him, but I reckon that I received my basic coaching from one of the greatest coaches the world has seen.'

Docherty played for English clubs including Preston North End and Arsenal and won 25 caps for Scotland. The principal reason for Docherty leaving Celtic (after making only nine first-team appearances) was that he generally played in the same position as Bobby Evans, the manager and the chairman simply failing to recognise his versatility and worth as a player. After his playing career, he was employed as coach with Chelsea, Barnet and Oxford University, and became manager of many clubs in England and Australia, including Aston Villa, Manchester United and Derby County. His managerial career included a year as Scotland's boss. In an interview given in 2003 Docherty commented 'These days we see players huddled together – bonding they call it – in the middle of the field before the game; well, Jimmy Hogan used to have them do that in the dressing room before we went out so it didn't cause any embarrassment on the pitch. The fact that his work was never properly recognised in this country says a lot about our attitude to coaching.'

Johnny Paton was equally complimentary:

> *Jimmy Hogan, when young, must have been a wonderful coach. I remember he was proud of his appearance, neat silver hair; he was always well turned out and immaculate. He was a practical coach because he could practise what he preached. It must have been frustrating for him because, even at the age of 65, he could still control, shoot and pass the ball perfectly. He probably was a better passer of the ball than Charlie Tully – and Charlie was our most gifted player by far.*

Like Tommy Docherty, Paton shakes his head at the opportunity wasted by several of Celtic's players:

> *Jimmy Hogan was in his late 60s when he came to Celtic, and he had lost a bit of his sense of discipline but none of his enthusiasm. Sometimes the practices would go on too long for the liking of some players. Professional footballers sometimes think that they know every aspect of the game just because they play for a big club. They are totally wrong...If he had been younger – or the players more*

*attentive — Celtic would have ended up playing the passing game perfected by Tottenham Hotspur in the 1950s — the famous 'push-and-run' style. That would not have been too wrong, would it?*

After leaving Brentford in September 1949, Paton went to Watford as player-coach. Later he became manager there, but his best work was as youth coach at Arsenal between 1961 and 1965, where he helped develop the backbone of their League and Cup double side of 1970–1971. When asked if Charlie Tully, the supreme individualist, was one of those who ignored their venerable coach, Paton replied:

*Charlie Tully certainly did not have a great attitude to training — at least to the monotonous grind of getting physically into shape: running laps round the track, climbing up the steps on the terracing etc. — but he respected Jimmy Hogan as a man. Both were devout Catholics and that was one bond between them. Charlie was a thoroughly decent human being, and he recognised what Jimmy Hogan was trying to do. Unlike some of the other established men, he would never make fun of him or criticise his methods. Charlie appreciated one thing the new coach initiated. During the previous season, whenever we asked for a ball at training, we would have got the reply 'What do you want a ball for? You'll get enough of it on Saturday.' Jimmy Hogan changed that way of thinking, and he was years ahead of his time in doing so. He would turn up at training with a string bag full of footballs — and we were like children scrambling to use them. Celtic wasted a wonderful opportunity. In England, men like Walter Winterbottom and Ron Greenwood (both England managers) followed his example. The West Ham Academy — with players like Bobby Moore and Martin Peters — was based on the coaching*

*initiative that Hogan had been teaching for years, but at Celtic Park too much was*
*left to the players on their own.*

Paton went on to point out that Jimmy Hogan was tireless in his approach to coaching, adding to his workload at Parkhead:

*Jimmy Hogan used to conduct clinics for supporters' clubs, and very often*
*Tommy Docherty and I accompanied him to demonstrate some skills — but we*
*had to be on our toes because the coach himself was an expert in the skills he*
*was teaching. We even went to Barlinnie Prison and, during the show when I*
*was not needed, I sat among the audience (to show that I was not stuck-up or*
*anything like that). To make conversation I asked the man beside me what he*
*was in for. 'Murder' was his reply — and for once I was relieved to be called*
*back up on the stage.*

An opportunity had been missed, but there were benefits from Hogan's time at Celtic Park. In general, Celtic's football improved on the pitch and some individuals found themselves as players. The most obvious example of the latter was Bobby Evans, who had been with the club since 1944 without ever finding his proper niche. Most often, he was employed as a makeshift forward, but he was fielded as right-half for the vital relegation battle at Dens Park on the last day of the 1947–48 season. Evans, apparently, assumed this was a one-off and had to be persuaded by Hogan that the midfield was his best territory. After the opening 12 matches of the new season and after Hogan's hands-on training, Bobby Evans had broken into the Scotland side, making his international debut at Cardiff in a 3–1 win over Wales on 23 October.

Another who developed, though not as dramatically as Evans, was Jimmy Mallan, who had been shifted around for seasons, either as right or left-back and frequently as centre-half. Such tinkering suggests a player not attaining his full potential but, in addition to these doubts, Mallan's temperament was highly suspect. In previous seasons he had been ordered off twice, and in those days a third sending-off could mean a lifetime ban; in fact, when he was ordered off in the notorious Victory Cup semi-final replay against Rangers in 1946, Mallan was suspended for three months. Hogan went to work on the troubled defender and succeeded to a certain extent as, before the end of the season, Jimmy Mallan received his only representative honour, being selected for the Scottish League against the English League at Ibrox on 23 March 1949.

Was Charlie Tully the sort of player to be coached? He had superlative skills: excellent and immediate control of the ball, a subtle style of dribbling and the ability to thread a pass through the most packed of defences. He would not have needed much improvement there, but Jimmy Hogan would have spotted two areas that required attention. Tully was a player sometimes guilty of over-elaboration, a tendency that had driven Elisha Scott at Belfast Celtic to distraction, and this was due to his undoubted talent. Why pass to a colleague who was likely to squander the opportunity presented to him? Why not hold on to the ball until an even better chance comes along? For a player recognised at the start of his days at Parkhead as an inside-forward, Tully was notably goal-shy and rarely broke through for a shot at goal. He considered himself more of a play-maker and was content to lay on goals for others.

One aspect remained that Jimmy Hogan was wise enough to ignore: Charlie Tully, as evidenced by the nickname 'Cheeky Charlie,' which had come with him from Belfast, was utterly unpredictable on the pitch, capable of attempting (and carrying out) the most outrageous of tactics. It was a gift from the football gods, and Hogan was astute enough not to interfere. As the 18th-century English poet Alexander Pope put it:

*Great wits sometimes may gloriously offend,*

*And rise to faults critics dare not mend.*

* * *

It was not going to be easy, in football or in real life. Even by August 1948 things had not returned to anything approaching normality in an austere Britain, still suffering food shortages and strict rationing; Princess Elizabeth, for example, had had to rely on donations of clothing coupons from ordinary Britons to get the material for her wedding dress in November 1947.

The football season, as usual, was the main topic of conversation among the sports-minded. Traditionally, Rangers held their Annual Sports event one week prior to the season, and even though several world-class athletes fresh from competing in the London Olympic Games were participating, many spectators were more interested in the five-a-sides. In fact on 7 August 1948, during the athletic meeting, Scotland's Alan Paterson and two American high-jumpers up from London were required to halt their contest while Clyde and Queen's Park finished their tie.

Charlie Tully was transferred from Belfast to Glasgow Celtic for the substantial sum of £8,000, but this did not raise too many eyebrows; ironically, a few months earlier, many letters were written by irate readers to the Glasgow newspapers complaining bitterly about the 'waste' of £8,300 to purchase Salvador Dali's masterpiece *St John of the Cross*. The painting remains to this day the most famous exhibit in the Kelvingrove Museum and Art Gallery.

To the delight (and possibly surprise) of Celtic supporters, Celtic won that meaningless competition at the Rangers Sports event, and the quintet left Ibrox just in time to participate in the club's pre-season public trial. It was an event usually played at exhibition pace, and this was no exception. In fact, the pace may have been further slowed by the effect of Celtic's new coach, the venerable Jimmy Hogan, whose approach was based on possession play and accurate passing. The players, regulars and reserves alike, gamely tried to keep the ball on the ground and pass to their teammates, manfully resisting the temptation to launch an attack with a hefty boot up the park.

Charlie Tully was not chosen for the competition at Ibrox but was presented to the fans at the trial match. He did not have the most impressive of starts. Apparently – and this may have been an indication of the generally slipshod approach to football in 1948 even at this high level – he had chosen to wear a new pair of boots. Footwear in the 1940s and 1950s was vastly different from now, and the boots (usually 'Hotspurs') had to be broken in carefully. Players tended to buy them one size smaller than their normal footwear and often chose to wear them standing in a hot bath to make the leather expand and mould to their feet. The famous Newcastle United forward Jackie Milburn used to break his boots in down the coal pit, in wet conditions. At any rate, boots were uncomfortable; the player got blisters, and a hobbling Charlie Tully was disappointed that he had not been able to shine in his first appearance at Celtic Park.

After three League fixtures, the League Cup started with its sectional play. This was a format highly regarded by the clubs, as it guaranteed at least six matches and often generated money. It was exactly the same as the present format in the Champions League (with the exception that only one club advanced from each section and that overall goal average was used to determine the winner if there was a tie on points). Celtic, who had frequently struggled in the competition, were drawn with Rangers, Hibernian and Clyde in their section – and there should have been little grounds for optimism. However, Celtic started with a 1–0 home win over Hibernian. The goal came in only three minutes when the visiting 'keeper Kerr could not deal with a fierce drive from Jock Weir near the corner flag. A week later, an all-ticket crowd of 25,000 packed Shawfield to see Celtic score early again, from Jackie Gallagher after two minutes and Willie Gallacher after 20. Following that bright opening, Celtic played sensibly and coped easily enough with Clyde's attacks.

And then came the match that made Charlie Tully's reputation in Glasgow. On 25 September 1948 Rangers came to Celtic Park and dominated play for the first 20 minutes. Findlay, a skilful poacher, swooped on a short pass-back to beat Miller in only eight minutes, but Celtic weathered the storm. Tully was being watched carefully by Ian McColl, and the Irishman started to wander in an effort to elude his marker but reappeared in his normal position to create the equaliser at 39 minutes. The *Glasgow Herald* reported 'Tully trailed half the Rangers' defenders with him, gesticulated to Paton exactly where the pass would go and served him perfectly. When Young (Rangers' centre-half) had to go for the winger, Gallagher had an easy task to shoot the cross through.'

One minute before half-time, Tully again prised open the Ibrox defence – the famed and feared Iron Curtain. Evans charged through on the right and crossed to Tully on the edge of the penalty area. Tully made no effort to control the ball but headed it into the path of Willie Gallacher, and Patsy's son steered the ball into the net from 10 yards. Normally, Rangers would have come out fighting but not this time. Celtic continued to press forward, with Evans and Tully controlling the midfield. Evans intercepted passes, tackled opponents and urged on his forwards in his trademark style. And Charlie Tully?

His was an amazing performance. He would gather the ball, kill it dead and then almost leisurely decide what to do with it. His first task was to taunt and humiliate his marker Ian McColl, and this he did in a variety of ways, leaving the Rangers' wing-half totally confused. Secondly, he continued to create havoc among the others in Rangers' defence. On one occasion 'the Irishman beat three would-be tacklers in the space of as many yards, and each time by a different manoeuvre. His ability was tantalizing, although that did not excuse the lunges made at him.' (*Glasgow Herald*, 27 September 1948)

After that breathtaking party-trick, Rangers' defenders appeared reluctant to approach Tully (never mind tackle him). Humiliation in front of a packed Celtic Park was too much to accept. In an Old Firm Cup tie, Tully was orchestrating the match and often reduced the game to a walking pace as Celtic strolled to a 3–1 win. It was this later development in the course of the match that was the probable start of the myth that Charlie Tully actually sat on the ball, with the Rangers defenders so demoralised that they were afraid to risk challenging him. This 'incident' did not happen, but it is an indication of Charlie's legendary status that many Celtic followers swear they did witness it. Even the Rangers supporters were impressed:

> *A week ago, at the close of the Celtic–Rangers clash, a crowd of 70,000 – and they weren't all Celtic supporters – lingered behind to applaud the magnificent performance of the smiling Irishman as he walked off the field. Little wonder. His slippery moves, coolness, cuteness, his apparent cheekiness on the ball stamp him as a truly great football craftsman. His very appearance on the field is a signal for a roar from the crowd.*
> (*Glasgow Weekly News*, 1 October 1948)

*Charlie is the smallest, as usual, on the left in St Kevin's team. (1934)*

*In action against Linfield. (1947)*

*The youthful Belfast Celt. (1947)*

*Celtic pre-Tully (1947):*
*Back row, left to right: Lynch, McMillan, Hogg, Miller, McDonald, Milne.*
*Front row: Quinn, Kiernan, Rae, McAloon, Hazlett.*

*Relegation battle at Dens Park: Patsy Gallacher with his sons, Tommy (Dundee) and Willie (Celtic). (1948)*

*Debut day for Charlie (1948):*
*Back row, left to right: Evans, Boden, McAuley, Miller, Milne, Mallan.*
*Front row: Weir, McPhail, Lavery, Tully, Paton.*

# CELTIC

**Official** **Programme**

JIMMY HOGAN

SCOTTISH LEAGUE
Saturday, 14th August, 1948
Kick-off 3 p.m.

## Celtic *v* Morton

PRICE 2d.

*The programme from Charlie's debut in Glasgow. (1948)*

*After training: Charlie, Jock Weir, Tommy Bogan and Jimmy Hogan. (1948)*

*Charlie's first 'cap' after three months in Glasgow. (1948)*

*His best match! Charlie and Carrie on their wedding day. (1948)*

*Miller, Evans and Milne get set...*

*Evans, Fallon, Collins and Fletcher run up Ben Lomond…*

*Collins, Weir and Fernie pitch in.*

*Sammy Cox (Rangers) duels with Alec Boden. (1949)*

*Danny Kaye meets Charlie (and Bobby Evans). (1949)*

*Consternation among the Lazio defenders as Charlie Tully's corner swings into the penalty area. John McPhail looks hopeful of adding to the four goals he scored that night. (1950)*

*Pals on and off the field: Charlie and John McPhail take part in training and celebrate a Scottish Cup triumph. (1951)*

# THE SCOTTISH FOOTBALL ASSOCIATION, LTD.

RCD/JKT

PATRON:
HIS MAJESTY THE KING.

SECRETARY:
GEORGE G. GRAHAM, O.B.E., J.P.

TELEPHONE:- SOUTH 2718-9
TELEGRAMS:-"EXECUTIVE, GLASGOW"

48 CARLTON PLACE,

GLASGOW, C.5.

J. McGrory, Esq.,
Celtic Park,
GLASGOW, S.E.

13th November, 1951.

Dear Sir,

              re C. Tully.

       With reference to my letter of 8th inst. I have to inform you that this matter will be dealt with by the Referee Committee at their meeting on Wednesday, 21st November at 3.30 p.m. when please instruct the above player to attend or send a written statement in his defence.

              Yours faithfully,

              Geo. G. Graham

                Secretary.

*An invitation from the SFA after being ordered off. (1951)*

*The Irish tricolour above 'The Jungle'. (1952)*

*Alec Rollo's lob beats Niven; Charlie and George Young watch. (1952)*

*Mr and Mrs Stein (and Charlie) with the Scottish Cup. (1954)*

*Celtic's other Irishmen: Sean Fallon is first off the plane and Bertie Peacock leads out Celtic.*

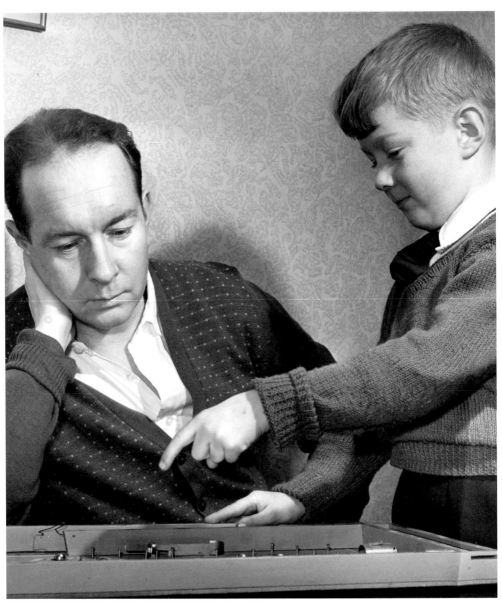

*A family man.*

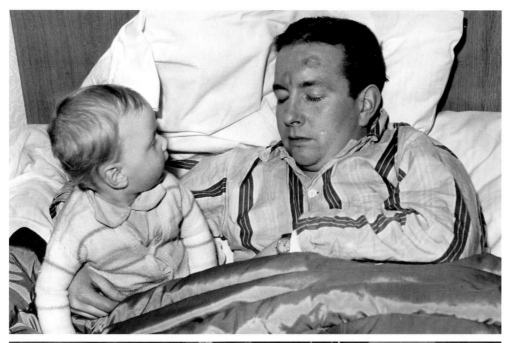

*Charlie Tully Jr gets to try on an Irish 'cap'.*

The headlines said it all: 'TULLY SHOWED GREEN LIGHT' (*Sunday Express*, 26 September 1948) and 'TULLY: BRILLIANTLY TANTALISING, TANTALISINGLY BRILLIANT!' (*Sunday Mail,* 26 September 1948). Tully's most memorable performance signalled the end of his freedom; the man who had wrecked and humiliated football's strongest and best-organised defence would now be a marked man on the pitch – and sought out off it. It was three wins out of three in the League Cup, and things looked good for this 'new' Celtic.

One week later, in front of a record crowd of 53,000 at Easter Road, the first indication of frailty came when Tully appeared as Celtic's inside-left but was shadowed by Hibernian's Sammy Kean, playing nominally at left-half. Kean was a wily veteran, a scrupulously fair player, and he never left Tully's side. In an effort to change things around, Tully switched to inside-right – but Kean also changed his position. It was a fair enough tactic, and it worked for Hibs at Easter Road, but other wing-halves in Scotland would prove less sporting than Sammy Kean. Celtic lost that return match at Easter Road by 4–2, with a resurgent Hibernian scoring three goals in the last 24 minutes.

On 9 October Celtic's bubble burst when Clyde visited Celtic Park. The Shawfield side took ruthless advantage of absences in Celtic's line up. Alec Boden had picked up an injury at Easter Road. His place was taken by debutant John McGrory, a gangling youngster who 'would play for Scotland one day', according to chairman Bob Kelly in one of his more romantic moments. The other absentee was Charlie Tully, off making his debut for Northern Ireland in a 6–2 loss to England. It was a shambles as Celtic, disorganised in defence and lacklustre in attack, had no answer to Clyde's thrusts and lost 6–3. McGrory could not contain Clyde's South African centre-forward Ackerman, who repeatedly drew the youngster out of position, while the forwards displayed neither guile nor penetration. Would things have been different had Tully been available?

The deciding match was played before 105,000 at Ibrox on 16 October, and among the spectators was Eamon de Valera, the President of Eire, invited there by Rangers during his state visit to Scotland. He did not appear to be much of a football fan, as he turned up about 30 minutes after the kick-off and left before the end of the match. Perhaps his entry and exit were staged to avoid any possible crowd trouble.

Rangers made changes from the first match at Parkhead. Woodburn had returned after suspension, and Cox was switched from his normal left-half position to right-half, replacing Ian McColl, where his task would be to mark Charlie Tully. McColl had been dropped, presumably for dereliction of duty during the 3–1 loss at Celtic Park, and remained out of the Ibrox side for several weeks.

It was an open match with even exchanges throughout the first half, but Rangers took the lead with a truly bizarre goal at 39 minutes. Alec Boden, in command of the situation, could have passed back to Miller advancing from his goal but elected to turn and clear the ball. Williamson, Rangers' centre, blocked the clearance, and the ball rose in an arc from some 40 yards out and flew over the head of the stranded Celtic goalkeeper. John McPhail equalised from the penalty spot four minutes into the second half, and a gripping match was decided with a splendidly executed breakaway goal by Willie Waddell, who outstripped the Celtic defence before lashing a diagonal shot past Miller.

Charlie Tully? He had a quiet match being watched closely by Cox, but he remained the creative source of Celtic's attacks. Celtic had to face the fact that Rangers had proved too strong and resilient; a lesson in character and in 'winning ugly' still had to be learned at Celtic Park.

The Glasgow Cup Final in September marked Celtic's return to respectability in Scottish football after years of disappointment. It should be noted that the Glasgow Cup was a highly sought-after trophy and, coming early in the season, it often produced acceptable attendances. The 1948 competition attracted record crowds, and the presence of Charlie Tully in Celtic's line up was a major factor — as noted in the *Glasgow Herald* account of the Final on 28 September: 'A queue eight-deep stretched from Platform 10 to the bottom of the Central Station and back up the carriage way. Six football specials had been arranged, but two more were called into action. Many holiday-makers wanted to go along to Hampden Park because they had never seen Charlie Tully in action.'

On that holiday Monday, an astonishing crowd of 87,000 turned up to see Celtic play Third Lanark — an indication that Celtic had turned a corner. The transfer fee of some £8,000 for Tully now seemed a bargain. In Celtic's progress to the Final, remarkable attendances had been the norm: 35,000 for a first-round tie against Partick Thistle, 51,000 for the replay and 31,000 for the semi-final against Queen's Park. Celtic's campaign had been eventful. The reluctance of the forwards to shoot and finish off their excellent work in the outfield was one problem that emerged in Celtic's opening League fixtures, and newspaper criticism was mounting. The *Evening Citizen* was acidic: 'Goal nets were introduced in 1891; Celtic may just be wondering why,' and on the morning of the Partick Thistle Cup tie, the *Glasgow Herald* (23 August 1948) commented presciently on the goal drought: 'Some of these days the legions of Celtic supporters will be struck as with a lightning shaft, for one of their players will score a goal and it will be all that the sanest man can do to keep his reason.' The journalist must have been the recipient of admiring glances in the Parkhead press box, because Celtic did score (through Jock Weir) amid rejoicing and uproar on the terracing, but the game had to be abandoned after 69 minutes due to lightning and torrential rain, which flooded the pitch.

The tie was replayed on 8 September, and Celtic ran out narrow and nervous 2–1 winners, with Tully netting the winner from close range. It was an unusually productive period for Tully, not often regarded as much of a goalscorer. He scored against Albion

Rovers (3–3) on 4 September, against Partick Thistle (2–1) on 8 September and against Queen's Park (3–0) on 15 September. The newspapers – which did not deal in gossip and mindless speculation in the late 1940s – reported that he was being monitored by the Irish Football Association. He did actually gain his first cap against England on 6 November of that year.

Queen's Park, no longer in the top flight in Scotland, put up a gallant resistance in the semi-final at Hampden Park but eventually were no match for Celtic, who won 3–0. Charlie Tully scored the decisive second goal. According to the *Evening Citizen* (16 September 1948), 'Tully, body well over the ball, beat one, two, and then a third Queen's Parker inside the 18-yard line. And then he hit his only shot of the game – and it was the only shot Ronnie Simpson, who had already saved a Mallan penalty kick, just did not see.' In his first appearance at Hampden Park, a stadium he would often grace in years to come, he had scored a memorable goal. The Spiders' goalkeeper was Ronnie Simpson, who would win a European Cup medal and everlasting glory at Lisbon in 1967, and the same newspaper described his performance as 'young Ronnie Simpson's best-ever game for Queen's Park'.

Third Lanark were no pushovers in 1948. In the previous season (1946–47), they had been impressive against Celtic, winning 3–1 and 4–1 at Celtic Park and 3–2 and 5–1 at Cathkin, with only one loss (a 3–2 result at Parkhead in a meaningless League Cup tie). Their recent form was equally impressive and included a 4–1 win over Rangers in the other Glasgow Cup semi-final.

In that Glasgow Cup Final, Celtic were lucky to be only one goal down at the interval, as Third Lanark started off brightly and launched wave after wave of attacking football. Jimmy Mason prompted his forwards with a stream of probing passes, and Bobby Mitchell teased and tormented Roy Milne in a virtuoso performance on the left wing. Celtic's Willie Miller was at his very best in keeping the score down with a series of fine saves. The turning point came eight minutes into the second half when Mitchell's penalty kick thudded against Miller's right-hand post, rolled all the way along the line and flicked the other post before rebounding to safety. Tully had been very quiet until then, policed by Third Lanark's defenders, but he started to make an impact, prompting his other forwards with shrewd passing. Willie Gallacher netted the equaliser, Jock Weir scored with a long-range shot, which swerved in the Hampden sunshine to deceive the goalkeeper, and Weir headed in the third just before the end – an insurance goal to cover the risk of a Third Lanark fightback. The line up was as follows:

**Celtic:** Miller, Milne, Mallan, Evans, Boden, McAuley, Weir, W. Gallacher, J. Gallagher, Tully, Paton.

**Third Lanark:** Petrie, Balunas, Kelly, Orr, Harrower, Mooney, Staroscik, Mason, McCulloch, Myles, Mitchell.

It had been a splendid match, a wonderful advertisement for Scottish football according to the newspapers. An evenly contested Final and an aesthetic delight, decided by the width of a goal post. Hampden Park, still deserving the title of the 'Classic Slopes' in those days, basked in the September sunshine, with most of the 87,000 crowd in shirt sleeves. The players' strips contrasted beautifully – the green-and-white of Celtic and the scarlet of Third Lanark – in the kaleidoscopic movement of attack and counter-attack.

For Celtic supporters (strange as it may appear to modern minds thinking of the Glasgow Cup), it marked a turning point. At last the club had won something meaningful; at last the team was playing attractive football; at last Celtic had a player worthy of comparing with giants of the past. Tully's influence on the pitch, despite his youth, and

Hogan's influence on the training ground, despite his age, were edging Celtic towards respectability. Bobby Evans continued to make progress under Hogan's guidance, as he won his first representative honour on 29 September when he turned out for the Scottish League in a 5–1 win over the League of Ireland. It was a heady five days for Evans, till then always promising but never quite fulfilling. He produced sparkling, energetic performances in victories in an Old Firm Cup tie, a Glasgow Cup Final and a League international.

Unfortunately, Celtic's improvement ultimately fell short of the highest standards as Celtic finished fifth in the League. Hindsight is always 20:20, but it was clear to many what the problems were at Celtic Park.

Footballers, when they reach the top flight in their national League, have a natural tendency to think that they have attained a level of professionalism – and this is perfectly natural. After all, these players have always been the best: in street football, at the public park, in schools football and in the juveniles and juniors. Little wonder that these young men considered themselves superior, and the adulation from family, friends and supporters would not help.

It was very difficult for any effective coaching to take place at this stage; the coaching should have taken place in the early days when good habits could be instilled. Jimmy Hogan, brilliant and well-meaning, could have only limited success with such players – and there were several at Celtic Park. Jock Stein, when he became Celtic's manager (and coach), knew what it was like to be a player and ruled with a mixture of fear and encouragement. No player was allowed to feel too important when he was in charge. Such stars as Billy McNeill and Jimmy Johnstone were occasionally dropped for a variety of reasons.

No such personality was present at Celtic Park in 1948 to ensure the discipline of true professionalism. The coach, Jimmy Hogan, and the trainer, Alec Dowdells, simply did not have the authority to enforce it; manager Jimmy McGrory – unlike Elisha Scott at Belfast Celtic – was a cypher, an absentee 'boss', described in the terracing phrase as 'Bob Kelly's office boy'; chairman Bob Kelly had the personality, the forcefulness and the authority to enforce his wishes. However, a lifetime of watching Celtic (and a few appearances for Blantyre Victoria) did not fully qualify him as the man to lead Celtic into the promised land. On the pitch, there was no player with the personality – the officer-material type – required to change things on the field through greater application; Bobby Evans and Charlie Tully were not that type. Both were outstanding, but Evans was still learning his trade and was not a natural leader. Tully was clearly an individualist, a man who relied on talent and moments of genius to turn games, but he was not the type of steady, reliable and organised team leader the situation required.

Even more importantly, some weaknesses were becoming more and more apparent, and it was clear that some players were not up to the standard required. In defence, Celtic did not have an organiser and the role of pivot was critical here. When Willie Corbett left Celtic in 1948, Celtic turned to various solutions to fill the gap: Alec Boden, Jimmy Mallan, John McGrory and even John McPhail. None of them was the right answer. Boden was a stopper centre-half and probably the best of this quartet, but he did not impose his personality on his fellow defenders; Mallan never appeared fully comfortable in the long run, although he could be useful as an emergency centre-half; McGrory was too impetuous and could be roasted by nippy forwards like Reilly (Hibs) and Mochan (Morton); and McPhail was too much of a footballer to concentrate solely on the mechanics of defending. Celtic had made enquiries a couple of years earlier about Belfast Celtic's Jackie Vernon, a commanding centre-half, but were frightened off by the thought of paying £8,500 for a defensive player. Vernon went to West Bromwich Albion, remaining a stalwart of the Northern Ireland international side and receiving the honour of representing Great Britain against Europe at Hampden Park in 1947. It was not until Celtic signed Jock Stein in 1951 that they obtained the sort of captain and model they required in defence.

The money for Tully had been largely raised by the transfer of Willie Corbett to Preston North End in June 1948. Significantly, Celtic had traded away their best organising centre-half in return for a forward. It was a frequent failing of Celtic team-building in the late 1940s and early 1950s. Forwards came and went, but Celtic did little to remedy the critical weakness in central defence.

Sadly, although it is in the nature of things, one of Celtic's better performers had started to exhibit unmistakable signs of decline. Willie Miller, Celtic's international 'keeper and so often a hero throughout the dreadful wartime seasons, was now becoming inconsistent, and his defenders had started to lack confidence in him. Jock Stein once commented that a great team requires a spine. Consider the Celtic team that won the European Cup, better known as the Lisbon Lions: Simpson in goal, McNeill and Clark in central defence, Auld and Murdoch in midfield, and Wallace, Chalmers (and McBride) as the strikers. The Celtic of 1948 had no such spine, literally and metaphorically, and the individual talents of such players as Charlie Tully and others would not be fully productive until this was remedied.

Celtic continued their quest for improvement but perhaps in the wrong direction: the board still pursued Wilf Mannion of Middlesbrough, although the north-east club were unwilling to sell, and they had to settle for Leslie Johnston from Stoke City. The former Clyde player, although a regular goalscorer, never appeared to be a settled player and always seemed ready to make himself available for transfer throughout his career.

At the end of the season, Celtic's report card would have been mixed: a promising start in the League Cup but ultimate failure…a barely respectable sixth-place finish in the League Championship, a mini triumph in the Glasgow Cup, a defeat to Partick Thistle after extra-time in the Charity Cup Final and, significantly, a shock defeat by lower division side Dundee United at Tannadice (4–3) in the Scottish Cup. Charlie Tully, however, had emerged as a leading player in the Scottish game on the field and off it. His skill, talent and a gift for the unexpected made him the idol of the Celtic support – and a talking point among supporters of other clubs.

Two instances might suffice: the highly expensive film *Bonny Prince Charlie*, starring David Niven and Margaret Leighton, had its premiere not in Scotland but in the Empire Theatre in Leicester Square on 21 October. Some of the historically challenged felt that it was based on Tully's life. Then, when the first child was born to Princess Elizabeth and Prince Philip, and named Charles, some people in Glasgow apparently believed he had been named after Charlie Tully.

Charlie Tully's arrival on the Scottish scene coincided with a massive increase in attendances and profits, and he could be considered the cause of that increase. In an austere post-war Britain still deprived of many basics, Charlie Tully provided colour and entertainment on the pitch. Off the field he was a journalist's delight, as he could provide an effortless stream of blarney, delightfully delivered in an Irish accent. Celtic's partial recovery was another feature in the rise in attendances. The crowds, certainly at the start of the season in the League Cup, were truly astonishing: 70,000 at Celtic Park for the Rangers game and 105,000 at Ibrox, 55,000 for Hibs at Celtic Park and 53,000 at Easter Road, 51,000 against Thistle in the Glasgow Cup and 87,000 at the Final against Third Lanark, 49,000 at Tynecastle, 39,000 at Pittodrie, 25,000 at Shawfield for the Clyde game and 23,000 at Coatbridge for Albion Rovers.

# Chapter 6

# *The Worst of Times*

In training, Jimmy Hogan had done his best to instill the basics into his players, but this was not always well received by the more established members of the squad. Any improvement made by such players was through osmosis rather than through diligent listening and application. The constant problem at Celtic Park was the lack of discipline throughout the club as an organisation. The practical hierarchy was as follows: the chairman, Bob Kelly, who made appearances at the ground almost every day; the manager, Jimmy McGrory, who spent most of his days in an office and rarely watched training; the coach, Jimmy Hogan, and the trainer, Alec Dowdells, who supervised the training sessions. Jimmy Hogan, as Johnny Paton has indicated, was past his best and struggled at times to keep the attention of several senior players. Alec Dowdells, a most amiable man and skilled at helping players achieve fitness, was no disciplinarian. Accordingly, training was often less than dedicated. Several players have pointed out that the tempo and application stepped up when the participants spotted Bob Kelly on the touchline or sitting in the stand observing them.

One paragraph in Tully's autobiography struck me when I first read it in 1958: 'One thing about Paradise and all who dwell therein – you are always good for a laugh. That's what's wrong with Rangers for instance. They have some decent lads on their playing staff, but they go around as if they had toothache. Not laughing, or even smiling. Dunno how they do it.' Most Celtic supporters would have preferred less laughter and more silverware. The fact is that Rangers had a core of hardened professionals, men who imposed a collective will on events; a team that salvaged draws out of losses and victories out of draws. Celtic did not possess that steel. In Bill Murray's *Glasgow's Giants,* the Australian academic puts it bluntly: 'Even if he had been a Protestant,

Charlie Tully would not have lasted two weeks at Ibrox.' It was frustrating to be a Celtic supporter in those seasons, as talent and flair were present in abundance at Celtic Park, and great results could be achieved on occasion, but form apparently depended on the mood and application of the players. Professional dedication was missing. However, after the improvement shown by Celtic in Charlie Tully's first season, Bob Kelly was in a cheerful mood at the start of the 1949–50 season: 'Only the best will do. The players who are honoured to wear the green-and-white, made famous on so many historic fields by their gallant predecessors, must realise the great traditions they are asked to uphold.'

Optimism is seldom in short supply among Celtic's supporters, but it was surely ill-founded for 1949–50. For the season opener – a League Cup tie against the traditionally formidable Rangers at Parkhead – Celtic were forced to introduce two raw and untried wingers (Bobby Collins and Mike Haughney who had played in the junior ranks for Pollok and Newtongrange Star the previous campaign). Before a crowd of 71,000, Celtic played well and with great spirit to win 3–2 in the August sunshine. In midweek, Celtic travelled to Pittodrie and prevailed in an exciting contest by 5–4. It was an excellent start to the sectional play in the League Cup, and Celtic were confident going to Paisley to face a St Mirren side who had lost 5–1 at Ibrox on the same Wednesday.

Despite the impressive start, the realists were not entirely convinced, and the inevitable downturn came at Love Street, where St Mirren fully deserved their 1–0 victory. To be honest, St Mirren could have won by more, as they had a goal disallowed and Willie Miller saved a penalty kick. The key match, therefore, would be at Ibrox on 27 August before an all-ticket crowd of 95,000. Both teams were level in points, but Rangers enjoyed an advantage on goal average – the method then in use to separate teams that were level on points.

Celtic started brightly enough, and young Haughney, clean through, smashed his shot against the crossbar, but an 'incident' took place at 30 minutes. As a spectator with a perfect view, I can recount at first hand what happened: the ball was running through to Brown in Rangers' goal, and Cox, Rangers' right-half, was shielding his 'keeper from Tully, who was following up and hoping for some mix-up. As Brown gathered the ball, Cox wheeled round and kicked Tully in the pit of his stomach. Tully went down a few yards from Rangers' goal, and everybody at the Celtic end of the ground, where the assault (and there is no other word) took place, anticipated the award of a penalty-kick and the ordering-off of Cox. Brown hesitated briefly but kicked the ball downfield, and Cox trotted out of his penalty area. Meanwhile, Tully rolled behind the goal in pain, and the referee (a relatively unknown official, R.B. Gebbie) waved his hands, allowing play to continue.

Pandemonium broke out behind the Rangers goal. Bottles flew, thrown by Celtic supporters, and landed among other Celtic followers near the front of the packed terracing[1], fist fights broke out, police re-enforcements rushed to quell the disorder, ambulance men appeared to tend to the injured and Tully still lay writhing behind the goal. Bobby Brown commiserated with him as the Celtic trainer raced round the track towards the goal, and the game still went on for a few more minutes! Finally, after more and more spectators had moved from the terracing to the relative safety of the running track, to be treated by St John Ambulance men or arrested by police, the match was halted. It took several more minutes for order to be restored and, after prolonged treatment from the Celtic trainer, Tully was able to resume, hobbling. Shortly afterwards, both Cox and Tully appeared to be cautioned by the referee for what seemed a trivial flare-up.

After the crowd scenes, the game took on a secondary importance and Rangers won 2–0, with Celtic playing disciplined football but at exhibition pace.

Without exception, the newspapers were sympathetic to Charlie Tully in this particular incident. The *Glasgow Herald* was scathing in its match report on the Monday: 'There is no doubt at all as to what caused the trouble – the foul committed by Cox, Rangers' right-half, on Tully, Celtic's inside-left, after 30 minutes' play, and the astonishing attitude of the referee in ignoring the offence and actually waving play on.' Also, a cartoon appeared in the *Evening Citizen* (9 September 1949) depicting an outraged referee declaiming 'As soon as a player gets kicked, he'll have his name took! An' if it happens again, aff he goes!' It is hard to avoid relating the cartoon to the Cox–Tully incident at Ibrox.

As a club, Celtic were rightly concerned about the consequences. In the past, Celtic Park had been closed for trouble attributed to Celtic supporters at both home games and away; in fact, the last occasion had been after a similar bottle party at Ibrox in 1941. The fans were incensed at what they perceived as incompetence – or worse – on the part of the referee. Accordingly, they requested that the SFA hold an inquiry into the causes of the disturbances at Ibrox[2].

The Referee Committee of the SFA released its report to the newspapers on 7 September, about three weeks before submitting it to the SFA Council: 'The Committee is satisfied that the rowdyism on the terracing was incited by the actions of two players, S. Cox (Rangers) and C. Tully (Celtic), and also in some measure by an error of judgement on the part of the referee.'

What was the 'error' that the referee had committed? It had to be his failure to award a penalty-kick for the foul on Tully and to punish Cox (and his team) for the offence. I have yet to meet a Rangers supporter willing to deny that a blatant foul was committed within their penalty area by Cox. I have also scanned the newspapers and not one has suggested any doubt existed about the offence. Such unanimity is conclusive. An offence – virtually an unprovoked assault – was committed on Tully by his immediate opponent in full sight of almost everybody within the stadium, with the exception of the referee and his nearer linesman. Critics pointed out that Cox, generally described as 'a tigerish ball-winner in midfield', had been switched from his normal left-half position to mark Tully. Perhaps he had misunderstood his task of 'marking Tully'. The Referee Committee stated unequivocally that the referee had made an error but fell short of describing it. Officialdom does tend to cover up embarrassing moments with vagueness, but what 'action' had Tully made – apart from being fouled by Cox in the penalty area? And how had that contributed to the deplorable scenes behind the goal?

In the Referee Committee judgement of 7 September, several recommendations were made: the punishment should be shared equally between both clubs; both were ordered to post warning notices on their grounds whenever they met in competition; both were ordered to post notices in their dressing rooms, drawing the players' attention to their responsibility on the field; and both players (Cox and Tully) were reprimanded and their records amended accordingly. The referee was informed that his failure to take appropriate action could have precipitated a more serious situation but, because of his previous fine record, no more action was contemplated against him.

Had 'appropriate action' been taken (a penalty-kick and the sending-off of Cox), there almost certainly would have been no trouble with the Celtic supporters. Why was Tully officially reprimanded? Certainly Cox should have been – as would have been the case had the referee performed his duty – but what had Tully done? Some have suggested that he exaggerated the degree of injury he had received, but this had never been part of his make-up as a player previously, nor would it be in the future.

The match was not televised nor filmed; accordingly, there was no 'evidence', leaving only the newspapers and eyewitness accounts to be considered. Without exception, every press account stated that Sammy Cox kicked Charlie Tully in the penalty area in front of the Celtic support massed at the Broomloan Road end of Ibrox Park. However, regardless of the provocation, it was the Celtic support who had behaved disgracefully – and Rangers may have had the right to feel aggrieved at having to warn their supporters (who had behaved impeccably, after all) about their conduct. It was yet another instance of the SFA's practice of apportioning blame equally and calling it 'justice'. The error by the referee should have been identified specifically, Sammy Cox – especially after admitting his culpability before the Referee Committee – should have been suspended, Charlie Tully should have been cleared of any suspicion of misconduct and Celtic should have been punished for the scenes involving their supporters.

The last recommendation put forward by the committee was an intriguing one: '...it would be advisable in matches such as those between these two clubs where tension is likely to be great to appoint a referee from another British Association.' Celtic had been claiming for decades that refereeing in Scotland was unsatisfactory, and this recommendation unexpectedly had proved the point.

Celtic were far from satisfied with the findings of the committee and especially the slur on Tully's reputation. It was a reaction shared by most of the objective followers of the sport: 'If ever a committee had an opportunity to exercise its authority here it was, but their decisions, to my mind, are a shirking of a straightforward duty' (*Daily Record*, 9 September 1949); 'The spectators saw Cox's action. If Tully provoked that action in a manner not apparent to the crowd, why have the Referee Committee not made public his share in the incident? Their finding implies that both players were equally to blame; that, so far as those who saw the incident can reason, was not the case' (*Glasgow Herald*, 10 September 1949); and 'The referee trouble, on the other hand, is a real headache. I know of only one referee on the list today who imposes his personality and ability upon the players from the start, and he has not been given a Rangers–Celtic game for eight years' (*Sunday Mail*, 18 September 1949).

Before the decisive SFA meeting on 26 September, the situation had become further inflamed as a consequence of a Glasgow Cup tie at Celtic Park on 13 September involving the same teams, meeting for the third explosive time in the month-old season. The atmosphere was tense, but both sides settled down to play attractive, open football and, consequently, the spectators – supervised by an increased police presence – settled down. In the first half John McPhail opened the scoring from the penalty spot, but Billy Williamson equalised with a neat header shortly after the restart.

Only two minutes remained in a match sportingly played by both teams when the referee (Mr W. Davidson) made the first of several sequential decisions that enraged the Celtic players and bewildered the spectators. He judged that Roy Milne, Celtic's left-back, had handled the ball about 10 yards outside the penalty area. It was a highly debatable decision, with most newspapers suggesting that the full-back had chested the ball. Celtic players, who had accepted every decision without question up to that point, surrounded the official to protest, although the incident had not taken place in a particularly threatening spot. The protests were prolonged, and the referee had some difficulty in extricating himself from the posse of Celtic players surrounding him. Meanwhile, one Rangers player decided to take the free-kick and passed the ball to Willie Findlay, suspiciously in the clear. The inside-right moved in on Miller in Celtic's goal (probably the only Celtic player not arguing with the referee) and slipped the ball past him.

Rangers followers (in the far end of the ground) celebrated the 'goal' with delight, but that turned very quickly to amusement at the events unfolding on the pitch. My own impression was that they were experiencing a form of collective embarrassment, as so often in recent seasons they had been accused by supporters of other clubs (and occasionally by the press) of enjoying favouritism from referees. One more instance just might be too much to explain away.

At first, Celtic supporters were not too outraged. They were irritated at Rangers taking such a quick free-kick without the referee's knowledge, but assumed – reasonably enough – that the referee would order it to be retaken. Annoyance turned into disbelief when the referee, whose back was to the actions of the Rangers players, turned round just in time to witness Findlay's finish and awarded a goal. He had given a dubious free-kick, had not signalled for it to be taken, had not been aware that the kick had been taken yards away from where the 'offence' had occurred and yet allowed the 'goal' to stand![3] Squads of policemen suddenly appeared from behind the stand and took up position on the running track to forestall any pitch invasion. There was none – simply because the Celtic supporters could not accept the surreal quality of the situation. After the events at Ibrox involving Celtic's best player, nothing would have surprised those supporters; outrage, it appeared, had been spent. The indignation on this occasion was a knee-jerk response to an utterly expected development.

However, events were unfolding on the pitch. Rangers players lined up in their half of the field, talking among themselves but ready for the restart. The Celtic players were arguing with each other, and it was clear what the discussion was about: some were indicating in speech and gesture that the whole team should walk off the pitch in protest at the decisions made by the referee. 'The ball was kicked away from the centre of the field as a gesture of dissent and, for a moment, it looked as if one [Celtic] player was encouraging the team to leave the field. The SFA can take action only if the referee's report calls for action' (*Evening Citizen* 14 September 1949). It was the custom in reporting matches in those days not to identify individual offenders, but it has to be said that Charlie Tully appeared to be the most involved in trying to persuade his colleagues to leave the pitch. It would have been a fatal mistake, but it would have met with the wholehearted approval of almost all the Celtic supporters in the ground, as they started to chant 'Go off!

Go off!' Only weeks into a new season that had seen Celtic beat Rangers 3–2 on the opening day, Bob Kelly was hearing some of the club's most loyal supporters shout out to him: 'Celtic should do a Belfast Celtic! Just get the hell out of football altogether!'

Common sense eventually prevailed and the game resumed. Rangers cleared Celtic's first attack after the restart, and the ball was punted down the right wing in the general direction of Waddell, their winger. Alec Boden, Celtic's pivot, raced over to deal with the situation, but his tackle on the Scotland right-winger was waist-high. Fortunately, Waddell had seen it coming and leapt high in the air to avoid it. Seconds later – although more than a minute remained to play – the referee whistled for the match to end. It was the one mature decision he had made in the closing stages of this Cup tie. The handshakes between the teams were sincere, and it was clear that most of the Rangers men were actively sympathising with their rivals.

The Celtic directors were more concerned (initially) at the conduct of the players in the incident. Several were called in to face the board and asked to explain their actions in delaying the restart and in disputing the award of the free-kick. Cyril Horne, the football correspondent of the *Glasgow Herald* and a man privy to the thinking of Celtic directors, told me some years later that the chairman was furious: 'He felt that the behaviour of the men on the pitch had taken away from the merits of Celtic's case against the standard of refereeing. It would become much more hard to convince SFA members of the validity of their complaints when their own players had been on the brink of walking off the pitch because a decision had gone against them.' Horne added with a rueful smile, 'Of course, Bob Kelly agreed with his players that it had never been a foul and that the goal never should have stood.'

Charlie Tully was examined in particular about his part in the hold-up in restarting the match – a delay that, in view of the events at Ibrox, could have led to a repetition of crowd trouble on a massive scale. By then, the directors had received inside information about the referee's report to the Glasgow FA, which criticised the Irishman 'for inciting his team to leave the field before the conclusion of the match'. It could not have been comfortable for Tully at that meeting with the directors. A street-smart boy from Belfast, he recognised instinctively that Bob Kelly was the man to appease. Charm would not work on Bob Kelly; repentance and reassurance about future conduct was required. Tully knew that he would not be left out of the side and left to rust in the reserves, but he could not discount the possibility that Bob Kelly would put him on the transfer list. Kelly, meanwhile, was a practical man, although he could be infuriatingly stubborn. He saw Tully as a great player and entertainer, a personality who had brought the crowds back to Celtic Park. He was a cult figure in the mould of Patsy Gallacher and Tommy McInally, but would he prove to be a genuine player or a mere entertainer?

Charlie Tully had been an ever present for Celtic from the start of the season until 17 September, but he was missing from Celtic's line up for the League game at Ibrox on 24 September and for the fixture against Raith Rovers at Parkhead the following week. For much of this time, Tully was in Belfast as Celtic announced that 'his muscle strain needs rest, and his wife is ill'. Very few believed this statement, assuming that Celtic had suspended him for his actions in the Glasgow Cup tie. The cynics pointed out that a muscle injury would receive better treatment at Celtic Park in Glasgow than on the Falls Road in Belfast.

Celtic had played Rangers three times since the start of the season, and the refereeing had been a talking point in each game. The SFA was the organisation in charge of the training and development of referees; the Scottish League, of course, was the principal employer of these referees. Astonishingly, officials of both bodies persisted in claiming that match referees were drawn by ballot, regardless of the importance of the fixture. However, shortly after this series of Old Firm matches, J.A. Mowat (Rutherglen) became virtually a fixture – a tacit, if belated, admission that the Old Firm required a mature referee capable of administering even-handed justice. Celtic – and in particular Bob Kelly – had no complaints about Mr Mowat's impartiality (although it was well known that he was an elder in the Church of Scotland). 'Waverley', the highly respected veteran of the *Daily Record* – a newspaper not considered a tabloid in the late 1940s – was blunt:

> *In the two most recent of this season's three games with Rangers, Celtic emphatically believe that they did not get justice from the referee. My opinion is that they were victims of weak refereeing. However, Celtic down the years have never believed that they were the sufferers of the controlling official's weakness as much as his prejudice. Indeed, there are responsible people connected with the club who go so far as to employ the word 'persecution'.*
>
> (12 September 1949)

Around this time, Brazil and Argentina were reported to be interested in obtaining three Scottish referees to officiate in South America. Their travelling expenses there and back would be taken care of, and the referees would get between £90 and £100 a month. Many Celtic supporters greeted the news with ill-concealed hilarity. The notes in the Celtic programme for the fixture against Hearts on 17 September made specific reference to the Glasgow Cup tie and were remarkably blunt about the refereeing decision(s):

> *...a splendid contest for 87 minutes, but then an amazing decision by the referee overshadowed all that had gone before...*

1. *Milne should not have been penalised because he did not handle the ball;*

2. *the kick was not taken from the proper place;*

3. *the kick was taken before the ball was dead;*

4. *the scorer was offside;*

5. *the referee did not signal for the kick to be taken. In fact, he had his back to the ball at the time...*

*We feel that this latest happening strengthens our claim to a special inquiry (into the events at Ibrox).*

Bob Kelly claimed rather ingenuously that Celtic were not complaining against recent specific decisions by referees. 'Celtic's concern was with the lack of control exhibited by referees,' he stated. Another body entered the dispute when the Scottish Professional Footballers' Union sent a letter to the SFA to express their concerns. In short, the union objected to the laying of blame chiefly on the players – and pointedly expressed dissatisfaction with the standard of refereeing and the organisation of referees. The clear implication in the letter was that referees should be constituted in an autonomous body and not directly affiliated to the SFA. Ironically, very few – if any – of the playing staff at Ibrox and Parkhead were members of the players' union, as the clubs did not approve of such activities.

The situation was complicated by the fact that Celtic and Rangers were due to meet yet again on 24 September. A day after the Glasgow Cup tie, the Celtic directors approached the Scottish League with an official request that this particular match be postponed 'until a more suitable time in the interests of public safety'. Their letter also made the suggestion that if the Scottish League felt the fixture should be cancelled altogether, Celtic would be agreeable to such an action; and, lest anybody might construe this as an attempt by Celtic to deprive Rangers of gate money, they would agree that the League match at Celtic Park on 2 January

1950 should also be cancelled. In those days the home clubs retained most of the money received at the turnstiles – at least in League fixtures.

Predictably, an outcry arose throughout Scotland: suggestions that Celtic were simply afraid of playing and losing to Rangers yet again were freely made, accusations that Celtic had slandered the reputation of Scottish referees were aired, and speculation that another outbreak of hooligan behaviour resulting in the closure of Celtic Park was rife. Even more bizarre was the rumour that Celtic were discussing the possibility of withdrawing from competition and closing down (as Belfast Celtic had done only a few months previously).

'Waverley' summed up Celtic's feelings: 'While the consensus is that the committee should turn down the request for a postponement, there is considerable sympathy for Celtic and there are clubmen to say that, in taking up the cudgels, the Parkhead club are fighting for clubs other than themselves. It appears certain that one good thing will emerge from the business – that the refereeing problem will be firmly tackled. And high time too' (*Daily Record*, 19 September 1949).

The Scottish League turned down Celtic's request, and the fixture was ordered to be completed as scheduled. It was around this time that Celtic imposed the 'unofficial' suspension on Charlie Tully and announced his 'injury', hoping to ease the tension of the occasion. The directors did not object too much when the Celtic Supporters' Association called for a boycott of the match as a protest. Bob Kelly spoke personally to the players and stressed the need for impeccable behaviour in this latest Old Firm clash. And what happened? Charlie Tully went home to Belfast to recuperate and have treatment for his 'injury'.

The attendance was estimated at 64,000 – a substantial decrease of 31,000 from the League Cup tie a month previously. Celtic were on their best behaviour, making only token tackles and avoiding physical challenges. Perhaps the one exception was Celtic's rugged right-back, Jimmy McGuire, who gave away a late penalty for a crude challenge on an injured Rangers player. McGuire had previously given away a penalty against Rangers on the opening day of the season. Bob Kelly acted promptly and dropped McGuire. The player made only one more appearance for Celtic and was given a free transfer at the end of the season. The difference between this treatment and that accorded to Charlie Tully is striking. Rangers won comfortably by 4–0 and the referee (M.A. Mann, Perth) had no difficulties in controlling players 'who would have paid homage to a schoolma'am refereeing a girls' hockey match' (*Glasgow Herald*).

The meeting of the full SFA Council was held on 26 September, and Bob Kelly, convinced of his player's innocence in this matter, moved that the minute should not be approved. In his speech the Celtic chairman, always a stickler for accuracy, pointed out a glaring inconsistency in the accounts (admittedly informal) that had circulated among SFA officials. It had been reported that the referee's view of the incident had been obscured and that he had been unable to see the offence clearly but, as Kelly pointed out, 'a high Scottish League official, not connected with any club, had questioned the referee at half-time and was told by the referee that he did not think the infringement committed by Cox was deliberate and that, therefore, he had ignored it'. The discrepancy should be cleared up, Kelly argued. Had the referee seen the incident or not? If not, why had a linesman not indicated whether an offence had been committed or not? Had Mr Gebbie told a League official that he thought any offence was accidental or not?

Despite Kelly's motion – and the weight of public opinion – the SFA Council adopted the Referee Committee's minute, censuring Tully by a vote of 25 to five. The visibly relieved chairman of the Referee Committee, Mr Angus Forbes of Inverness, stated categorically and unwisely that 'Tully had simulated any slight injury he may have received.'

In recent times, spectators – either at football grounds or settled in armchairs at home and watching frequent TV replays – have become aware of an increase in the number of players who cheat in order to gain an advantage from the referee and/or to get an opponent into trouble. In 1949 such actions were rare, and Charlie Tully was never known as 'a diver' throughout his career with Celtic. Yet – in order to protect the reputation of a referee – this seemed to be the opinion of this particular Referee Committee, who were unwilling to extend the same courtesy to a footballer.

Where had these few weeks left Charlie Tully? His career was at a crossroads. He had broken into Belfast Celtic as a youthful prodigy and developed into a player of undoubted promise. After his transfer to Glasgow Celtic, he had emerged as a genuine star player, a charismatic figure…but now, after the match at Ibrox on 27 August 1949, it looked as if he had become a victim and, accordingly, a martyr for many within the Celtic support.

Tully's reception by the crowd at Celtic Park for the Hearts League fixture on 17 September confirmed his standing within the Celtic community, and his sparkling display that afternoon (only a few days after the trauma of the Glasgow Cup tie) only enhanced his status. It had been quickly recognised by opposition players that the best way to control Tully was to delegate a specific player to man-mark him; this was part of the game and accepted as such. The vicious foul by Cox at Ibrox Park was a disturbing development (and fortunately it would be a relatively isolated event), but Charlie Tully's career and future in Glasgow were at risk. Physically hurt on the field, publicly criticised and officially censured for it – and his offence lay in being fouled by another player. Already idolised by an adoring Celtic support, Tully was now elevated to the status of a martyr (and in his own wilful way, he had worsened the unhealthy situation by his actions in the Glasgow Cup tie).

## Notes

1.  I was a youngster at the time and, along with two teenage friends, was ordered at the turnstiles to drink my bottle of lemonade before being allowed to enter the ground. As several hundred bottles were hurled in the general direction of the pitch, the police were clearly less vigilant at other turnstiles.

2. For crowd scenes at Ibrox in 1941, which involved Celtic supporters, the SFA ordered Celtic Park to be closed for a month. Arguably, the trouble at Ibrox in 1949 was even worse. The police had made several arrests among the Celtic support congregated at the Broomloan Road end of the ground, and the offences included 'drunk and incapable', 'breach of peace' and 'falling asleep on the terracing'. At Govan Sheriff Court on the Monday, all were found guilty and fined (£1) or imprisoned (30 days). Another supporter was given 30 days for 'breach of peace' by throwing a bottle at a supporters' bus at Bridgeton Cross. The trouble did not end there: when Celtic travelled to Dumfries to play Queen of the South for the first League fixture, several followers were arrested and fined. They included one from Coatbridge who threw a bottle at a shop window, and another (from Glasgow) who jumped into River Nith declaiming 'I want to die!' and had to be rescued by police and fellow supporters.

   Following the replay of the Victory Cup semi-final in 1946 – during which four individual spectators invaded the field – three Celtic players were suspended by the SFA. George Paterson, ordered off for dissent, got three months; Jimmy Mallan, ordered off for kicking the ball away, also received three months; while Matt Lynch, neither ordered off nor cautioned, was suspended for a month. Celtic, therefore, were concerned about the reaction from the SFA.

3. I am more aware than most that this account of events could be interpreted as another example of 'Celtic paranoia', but I have to assure the reader that it is a factual account. I was in 'The Jungle' for this match and had a perfect view of the incidents described. In fact, I have refrained from adding that Findlay, the 'goalscorer', was almost certainly offside when he gathered the ball.

# Chapter 7

# The Scottish Cup – At Last

The last time the Celtic legions celebrated a Scottish Cup triumph had been in 1937, when Celtic defeated Aberdeen 2–1 before a record crowd of 146,433. That was 14 years previously, and a whole generation of Celtic supporters had grown up without seeing their team lift the trophy. It was the clearest indication of how far Celtic had slumped in those 14 years, but despite this fact, the Parkhead club still remained the record holders in the competition, with 15 triumphs. Charlie Tully's arrival and a marked improvement in on-field performance had raised hopes once again, but they had been dashed cruelly in the recent past. In 1949 a complacent Celtic had arrived at Tannadice to face Second Division Dundee United and left two hours later, thrashed 4–3 in an almost incredible upset; a year later, Celtic went down 1–0 to a resolute Aberdeen side at Celtic Park, a shade unluckily but out of the Scottish Cup once again. Celtic's hopes, as always in those days, were pinned on Charlie Tully, and perhaps it is time to visualise the Irishman as he was in 1951.

If Charlie was playing that day, the crowd would be quiet and attentive as the teams were read out. A great murmur of approval arose if John McPhail was considered fit to play at centre-forward and, if Charlie were picked at inside-left, nobody heard who would be playing on the wing such was the roar...and, if he were to be fielded at outside-left, the suspense would have been unbearable until his name was read out.

Taking his position prior to the kick-off, he is stared at, examined and scrutinised: *does Charlie look fit? Do you think he's in the mood today?* Sooner or later, the ball would be played in his direction. A sudden hush, anticipation rising. Acclaim if he gathers the ball quickly and cleanly, and roars as he races forward. *Is he going to get round that full-back, a big bruiser?* Groans if the defender tackles and wins the ball...satisfaction if Tully gains a throw-in out of the situation…a sense of muted disappointment if he decides to pass the ball, no matter how accurately…and jubilation, noisily expressed, if he gets past the defender with the ball, deceiving him with an almost imperceptible feint. The game goes on…howls of rage when he is tackled vigorously and downed…shouts of warning, rarely needed, whenever a would-be tackler approaches from behind…or head-shaking if Tully nudges an opponent or pushes him, invariably openly, as if wanting to be caught. Applause and appreciative calls from the more perceptive in the main stand or the enclosure at some typical dribble…and roars of approval from those in 'The Jungle'.

At times, alone on the wing, with the play going on elsewhere on the pitch, he seems forlorn, vulnerable even, hugging himself as if cold, with his collar turned up. You can see he appears frail, waif-like almost, until the ball arrives at his feet. Transformation. Ball under control instantly, he approaches the retreating defender. A suddenly apprehensive defender, trying to focus but wondering exactly what this unpredictable winger might attempt next. Whatever it will be, the full-back knows that he is to be the intended victim of sublime skill – or the butt of a joke. *He doesn't even look like a real player, with thinning hair and a bit of a stomach, and he's not even near 30 yet. He's not really fast, but he can leave you for dead if he gets past and can put a cross from the wing on to a sixpence, but you never can tell which way he's going to turn. A nightmare to deal with. A bloody chatterbox as well. Never listen to him. If you do, you'll want to answer, to get your own back – and you just can't win with a patter-merchant like him. What he says sticks in your mind, preys on it.* That was Charlie Tully in 1951, the star player in an inconsistent, underachieving Celtic side.

Shortly after New Year's Day, after a 1–0 defeat by Rangers – and with John McPhail injured with a groin strain, having slipped over-stretching for a pass on a dreadful Ibrox pitch – Celtic's hopes of a successful season started to fade. The League Championship was already out of reach, and only the Scottish Cup remained – but they had not won that since 1937.

The Cup draw had not been particularly kind, giving them a potentially difficult opponent in East Fife at Methil on 27 January 1951. Playing on their own pitch, bone-hard that day, the Fifers looked capable of an upset, especially as Celtic would be without McPhail at centre-forward and were shaky in defence. John Bonnar was badly at fault when a corner-kick from Black, on the right, escaped him and ended up in the net after 24 minutes, but Jock Weir equalised 15 minutes later, only for John Duncan – who had played for Celtic during the war – to smash in a fierce shot just before half-time.

The second half was a tense affair: Celtic were making an effort to get back into the game, but East Fife were resolute in defence. The Fifers looked dangerous in frequent counter-attacks, with Celtic's defenders uneasy on a treacherous surface. As the minutes passed, Celtic became more desperate, gaining corner after corner – but without John McPhail they lacked a spearhead. With eight minutes left, Charlie Tully gained the ball on the left wing near the corner flag. He rounded one defender, hesitating as if considering whether to gain yet another corner, but decided finally – amid shouts of impatience from the travelling support – to cross the ball. He delivered it perfectly, a couple of yards outside the goalkeeper's reach, and Bobby Collins – only 5ft 3in of him – reached it first to head it into the net. Celtic wisely concentrated on playing safe for the last few nervous minutes and left Fife with a 2–2 draw and a replay at Celtic Park.

Celtic welcomed back John McPhail for that replay, watched by 36,000, and, although he did not look fully fit, he scored twice in a 4–2 win. His presence inspired Celtic to a 4–0 lead by half-time. Another change for this Cup tie was the debut of George Hunter in goal. Like John Thomson before him, Hunter had made his first appearance for Celtic as a teenager and in a Scottish Cup tie.

The second-round draw pitted Celtic against Duns at Parkhead on 10 February, and it came as a welcome relief. It afforded more time for McPhail to recover and to rest

Tully for the more important matches ahead in the Scottish Cup; by then, the club had given up all hope of competing seriously in the Championship. An even more important change was caused by an injury in the East Fife replay to John McGrory, the centre-half; Celtic now called upon Alec Boden, who went on to play the best football of his career and to retain the position ahead of McGrory and Jimmy Mallan. The result was a comfortable 4–0 win over the non-League outfit, who had the consolation of a half share in the 22,907 gate.

On 24 February, Celtic went to Tynecastle to face a most formidable Hearts side, and young George Hunter played the game of his life in goal. During a first half dominated by Hearts – and faced with 'The Terrible Trio' of Conn, Bauld, and Wardhaugh – he held the Edinburgh side at bay almost single-handedly. Time after time, he stretched to divert raging shots and defy the home side. After 45 minutes of constant bombardment by Hearts, the teams trooped off at half-time, with Celtic leading 2–1. Celtic had made only two serious attacks but scored twice. Jock Weir scrambled home the first after Brown had parried a shot by McPhail, but the winning goal was a mini-classic. Hunter gathered the ball and threw it down the left touchline to Charlie Tully, still inside his own half. Neatly, he and John McPhail cross-passed their way down the pitch to find space within the defenders. Tully's final pass found McPhail alone near the penalty spot, and the centre-forward's delicate touch clipped the ball past Brown, completely isolated and stranded a few yards out of his goal. That goal – and Hunter's gallantry – completely broke Hearts, and Celtic coped reasonably comfortably throughout the second half to advance and meet Aberdeen in the next round.

Aberdeen had beaten Celtic in both League fixtures (2–1 at Pittodrie and 4–3 at Celtic Park), but expectation was rising within the Celtic support. Controversy broke out before the game when it was revealed that the referee (Mr J.A. Mowat) had received death threats in the event of a Celtic defeat. The attendance was announced as 75,000, but Celtic Park was packed long before the kick-off, so much so that the police allowed hundreds of youngsters to sit on the track behind the goals.

Celtic dominated the play with both McPhail and Tully in top form, despite doubts about their fitness and availability beforehand.[1] At 15 minutes, Tully laid on a chance for McPhail, who netted from close range. McPhail reciprocated a few minutes before half-time, and Tully calmly beat Martin, Scotland's tallest goalkeeper, from 10 yards out. Near the end of the second half, John McPhail scored again to round off a perfect day for Celtic – and Mr Mowat returned to the safety of his Rutherglen home, unworried about any repercussions.

The semi-final against unfashionable Raith Rovers at Hampden Park was an absorbing affair. Twice Celtic took the lead (through Weir at seven minutes and McPhail at 40), and twice the Fifers fought back (a Boden own-goal at 35 minutes and Penman at 80). Throughout the match, Charlie Tully had tormented McClure, the Rovers right-back, twisting and turning and totally confusing the defender who, as always, played him cleanly – before crossing into dangerous areas. In addition, his distribution was impeccable and every move threatened Raith Rovers' goal. Indeed, many astute observers believe this performance was Charlie Tully's best in a Celtic jersey.

With the game poised at 2–2 with seven minutes left, Celtic gained a free-kick down the left touchline, about 10 yards inside Rovers' half. Joe Baillie hoisted the free-kick towards the far post, where it hung in the air. McPhail, Colville and Johnstone (the goalkeeper) went for it and collided. The ball broke from the mix-up and Tully was quickest to react, as he prodded it into the net for the winning goal. Celtic were jubilant, but Raith Rovers were furious, claiming that McPhail had impeded both the centre-half and goalkeeper to allow the ball to reach Tully, and they did seem to have a case. However, Celtic were in the Scottish Cup Final for the first time since the 1930s and would face Motherwell.

On a bright, sunny day the Hampden pitch was fast and fiery. Control was difficult, and nerves played a part in a Cup Final that never reached the heights expected. Even the skilled players like Charlie Tully and Johnny Aitkenhead struggled to make an impact. The first great moment came at 12 minutes when John McPhail burst through the middle to draw the 'keeper from his line and chip the ball past him; the second was at the end when the Celtic support – who had been whistling for the previous three or four minutes to encourage the referee – erupted with joy when Mr Mowat took the hint. Charlie Tully and John McPhail, the heroes of the campaign, embraced, and Celtic supporters exulted in the belief that the wilderness years were over.

## Note

1. I have a clear personal memory of this match. I had made a point of arriving early, and was walking along London Road towards the ground about 90 minutes before the kick-off when I heard a stir behind me. There, walking along, were John McPhail and Charlie Tully, both looking very confident and fit – particularly McPhail, who appeared 'as brown as a berry'. Many supporters were walking alongside, careful to avoid jostling the two stars and giving them room on the crowded pavement.

# Chapter 8

## *An Antic Disposition*

Charlie Tully was described often as 'a cheeky chappie' or 'a jester'. Sometimes in the convoluted vocabulary of sports writers in Scotland, he was described as 'a character'. Basically, all three terms mean much the same – and more importantly they are accusatory, negative in tone, the implication being that the player has substituted outrageous behaviour for skill and effort.

In the 1920s Tommy McInally was exactly such a personality – a potentially outstanding footballer whose talent was never fully realised, a performer who believed that entertainment consisted of him showing off with the ball. For him, professional football was not a job, and team play was a hypothetical topic. One Celtic historian stated, however, that if Celtic were indeed 'a family club' then Charlie Tully's father would be Tommy McInally (and his son would be Bertie Auld). An interesting and amusing concept.

Apart from sharing an inordinate core of talent and ability to attract attention – and become popular and accepted among Celtic supporters – there might be little comparison between McInally and Tully. To be blunt, if not cruel, Charlie Tully sometimes played the clown if he felt the occasion warranted it; Tommy McInally was a clown. There was, however, another connection between the two personality players and it came upon Tully's arrival in Glasgow from Belfast in 1948. As a relatively innocent newcomer to the city, he found his way to the Bank Restaurant, a well-known 'howff' run by Willie Maley, who had spent virtually a lifetime (from 1897 to 1940) as Celtic's secretary-manager. There, the newcomer met the 80-year-old Maley and Tommy McInally himself. Apparently, Tully asked for directions to Celtic Park, and McInally was quick to give him detailed directions – to Ibrox. As he had done so often in his career as Celtic's manager, Maley had to chide his wayward player (and point the young Tully in the right direction). During his Parkhead career, McInally frequently ran foul of the autocratic manager yet Maley had a soft spot for his player, and McInally could get away with saying things that would have resulted in others being suspended or transferred.

Tommy McInally came to Celtic from St Anthony's in 1919 and marked his debut on the first day of the 1919–20 season with all three of Celtic's goals against Clydebank. He followed that with two goals against Dumbarton in another 3–1 win. By the end of his first season, the teenage sensation had made 34 appearances and scored 30 goals. At that time he was basically a centre-forward, noted for his direct action and ferocious shot, but it was his personality, as well as his prodigal talent, that would be remembered by the supporters. He seemed incapable of being serious for too long, unable to resist the temptation for clowning either in training or in match conditions.

The Barrhead boy never developed into the genuinely great player he always promised to be, although Celtic switched him from striker to inside-forward so that he could demonstrate his sublime skills and reading of the game. He was often unpopular with his teammates, who resented the clowning which at times threatened their livelihood in the financially precarious years after World War One. In fact, he was severely criticised by everybody for his antics in the 1927 Scottish Cup Final against lowly East Fife, a match won 3–1 by Celtic. The Second Division Fifers had surprised everyone by reaching the Final, and Celtic were overwhelming favourites, so much so that manager Willie Maley reacted in disbelief to a request from his players to consider a bonus. 'A bonus for beating East Fife? Come on!' was his answer.

Tommy McInally's behaviour on the Hampden pitch that April afternoon, before more than 80,000 spectators, was equally dismissive. After Celtic had taken the lead, he clowned to his heart's content, holding the ball ad nauseam, trying out back-heels and compounding things by 'shooting' at goal from 40 or 50 yards instead of passing the ball to his colleagues. It was the most significant occasion on which the irrepressible Tommy overdid things.

Like Tully, he was a chatterbox on the field, unable to resist the wisecrack. Interestingly, it was reported that on one occasion when he was ordered off by the referee, who uttered the usual words 'To the Pavilion!' McInally allegedly pleaded with him 'Can you not make it the Empire? I went to the Pavilion last night and it wasn't a great show.' Almost exactly the same apocryphal story appeared in print and was circulated widely around Glasgow when Charlie Tully was sent off against Third Lanark on 3 November 1951.[1]

Astonishingly, Willie Maley, the grimmest of all managers, found it difficult to discipline McInally. It may have been his prodigious talent or genuine innocence, but McInally could get away with things that nobody else could at Celtic Park. However, Maley's patience or tolerance was exhausted by 1922, and McInally was transferred to Third Lanark. In his three full seasons he had played 101 matches and scored 78 goals, but this was not enough to save him. Simply, the player would not train and had become recognised as 'a first-half man'; no amount of skill could fully compensate for a lack of fitness – and at the age of 21! He was allowed to return to Celtic in 1925, greeted by Maley 'like a prodigal son', but the results were much the same and he lasted only another three seasons before his attitude forced Maley to transfer him again, this time to Sunderland. In this spell – where he was used primarily at inside-forward as a sort of general, he played 112 matches and scored 52 goals.

Despite these impressive statistics, his career must be considered a major disappointment, such was his natural talent. Twice the feckless McInally was to be considered the standard bearer for a 'new' Celtic and each time, his manager and his club were let down: in 1919–20, with the world in front of the young centre-forward McInally, Maley decided to let Jimmy McColl, a prolific scorer, depart. And in 1926, trusting that

McInally, after four years with Third Lanark, had matured as a person and had developed into an inside-forward, Maley decided to let the irreplaceable Patsy Gallacher go to Falkirk.

McInally's immaturity was shown a few days before a Scottish Cup tie at Fir Park against Motherwell (3 March 1928). A couple of players played a relatively innocent prank on him by pretending to be newspaper reporters interviewing him by phone. The gullible McInally fell for the trick and spoke at length to 'the reporter' who, of course, asked him for comments on his colleagues, and Tommy obliged. Apparently, everybody was in on the act and, upon catching on, McInally was so piqued that he walked out of the Seamill Hydro where Celtic were training and rendered himself unavailable for the Cup tie. Celtic's directors were so upset with this latest antic that they vowed McInally had played his last game for the club, but he was restored to the side after a month's absence – perhaps at the insistence of Willie Maley, who was hopeful of landing both the Scottish League and Cup. Unfortunately Celtic faded at the end of the season, and it was Rangers who lifted that double. There was no way back for Tommy McInally after this and he left for Sunderland, where astonishingly he was appointed captain in a vain attempt to help him become a more professional player.

\* \* \*

Charlie Tully was vastly different from Tommy McInally. Unlike the Celt of an earlier generation, Charlie's antics had a point and Billy McNeill for one is very specific about that: 'He was a player first, and then an entertainer.' He may not have read *Lifemanship* by Stephen Potter, but he certainly was an expert in 'gamesmanship' – a practice defined as 'the art of winning without actually cheating'. In his book, the English humorist describes what sports writers of Tully's generation called 'kidology', whereby 'Each of us can, by ploy or gambit, most naturally gain the advantage.' It is also based on the idea of 'How to be one up – how to make the other man feel that something has gone wrong, however slightly.' Tully was a master of such ploys and while, no doubt, they were done for practical purposes on the pitch, the Irishman gave the distinct impression that he actually enjoyed the process as well as the product. His idiosyncrasies were a direct result of his football intelligence because it was increasingly obvious that they were calculated to tease, goad or madden his marker into losing composure and rush into reckless precipitate action. No other forward in Scotland was more adept at exploiting that fatal split-second when irritation took over from judgement.

What forms did it take? The most obvious transgression was the taking of corner-kicks from a spot just outside the arc, but it was a ploy that almost backfired on the Irishman on the occasion of his twice-taken corner at Brockville in 1953. Such a practice can cause the defenders' concentration to waver for a split-second, and that was the clearest reason for Tully using it so often. I have a clear memory of Tully taking one corner at Celtic Park, placing the ball several **yards** from the corner flag and getting away with it; presumably the closer linesman was on the other touchline, and the other at the halfway line had assumed the referee had awarded a free-kick. While I cannot remember the occasion nor the opponents, the memory of Charlie's cheek remains clear. Sometimes the practice was irritating to purists among the Celtic support, but it was part of his makeup.

Does it work? Probably its value as an unfair advantage is often overrated but, having written that, I can remember the waves of anxiety swirling around Celtic Park when an AC Milan player placed the ball a few inches outside the arc in the latter stages of the October 2007 Champions League match. It certainly has a most upsetting effect on the crowd.

Another characteristic ploy was Tully's habit of gaining instant control of the ball by chesting it – a perfectly legitimate practice. But Tully had developed the habit of having his shoulders hunched forward and simultaneously pressing his arms close to his chest and a little bit forward from his body. Thus, the impression was often given that Tully had come closer to catching the ball than chesting it. An opponent appealing in vain for a free-kick for 'hands' against Tully could find himself at a disadvantage. Sometimes the referee sided with the defender and penalised Tully, but this seemed only to inspire the Irishman. Playing the role of the martyr somehow appealed to him, and an occasional free-kick in a harmless location was a small price to pay.

Sheer cheek was another component of Charlie's persona. One often-cited demonstration was the incident in the St Mungo Cup Final at Hampden Park in 1951. Celtic had started sluggishly and Aberdeen brightly; within 35 minutes the Dons were two goals up and controlling the game – until Charlie Tully took matters into his own hands. His first move was to change position by switching from his left-wing spot to take up a roving role on the right. One Celtic raid had ended with a throw-in about 10 yards from the corner flag. Tully moved to take it quickly but found no other Celtic player in position to receive it. Unabashed, Tully aimed the ball – not violently, it should be stressed – at the back of the retreating Aberdeen full-back. The ball struck the defender, Davie Shaw (the brother of Rangers' full-back and captain 'Tiger' Shaw), and went out for what Tully claimed as a corner-kick. To Tully's delight and to Shaw's annoyance, referee J.A. Mowat saw nothing wrong with the action and awarded a corner. Almost needless to say, Charlie Tully took the corner-kick, and Sean Fallon bundled the ball into the net, with the Aberdeen defenders still ruffled at the success of the gambit.

Celtic improved after this goal. Tully was lifted by the success of his ploy and roasted the Aberdeen right-back, the often fearsome Don Emery, throughout the second half. It was Tully's cross from the byline that enabled Jimmy Walsh to score the winning goal and, probably to Tully's secret delight, there seemed a question about whether the ball had crossed the line before he crossed it.

Quite often, and particularly in the opening minutes of a game and without any provocation, Tully would commit the most blatant foul on his immediate opponent: a two-handed shove in the back as he moved for a high ball was a recurring offence, harmless in that it did not cause any physical harm but vastly disconcerting to a defender unused to forwards taking the physical initiative. It would occur only once in a match, but its effect was apparent in the subsequent hesitancy of opposing full-backs, always mentally preparing for a repetition.

On 3 March 1956 one action of Tully's could be interpreted as coming close to 'cheating'. In a Scottish Cup tie at Celtic Park against an Airdrie side who had taken Celtic to a replay in the previous season's semi-final, Celtic took a deserved lead through Bobby Collins but gave up an equaliser midway through the second half. A replay against this Airdrie side at Broomfield was a daunting prospect, and Celtic piled on the pressure. With only 12 minutes left, Tully was fouled on the edge of the penalty area; it was a foul, no doubt about it, but Tully required treatment from the trainer – a rather prolonged treatment. I was in 'The Jungle' that day, and the man alongside nudged me and whispered 'Watch Tully! He's up to something.' I took the advice and saw Tully standing beside the Celtic player delegated to take the free-kick; he shook his head in response to some remark and remained doubled up in pain. Instead of shooting for goal, or crossing to the far post, the Celtic player – probably Collins or Peacock – rolled the ball two yards in front of the unmarked Tully who, having made a miraculous recovery, advanced several yards before sliding the ball past the Airdrie 'keeper for the winning goal. Cheating? It may have been sharp practice, but it was a free-kick and Tully did require some treatment from his trainer.

Talking was another ploy Charlie Tully used to disturb the concentration of opponents, no matter how celebrated. In writing a previous book (*The Glory and the Dream*, with Pat Woods) I wrote to Joe Mercer, the English manager, at his home in the Wirral. Pat and

I had noticed that the legendary wing-half had played against Celtic in the Empire Exhibition Trophy as an Everton player in 1938 and also against Celtic as an Arsenal player in the Coronation Cup of 1953. We thought his views might have some relevance. His reply was courteous and detailed; a fine letter from one of football's gentlemen. I can recall one sentence: 'In the Coronation Cup Celtic surprised us with their play – bright, attractive and adventurous and, of course, playing against Charlie Tully was an education in itself!'

Only one full-back seemed impervious to Charlie's chattering, and that was bluff Irishman Albert Murphy, who played outstandingly well for Clyde for a number of seasons. Perhaps he was immune to Charlie's engaging Irish lilt, because Tully could never interrupt this sturdy defender's concentration with small-talk and banter when playing against him.

The use of outrageous skill to leave an opponent floundering could well be described as a ploy where Tully was concerned. Imagine being the defender delegated to mark this man: slightly built, almost frail-looking, a rear end that jutted out incongruously and a top speed that could be described charitably as little more than an ungainly gallop...but with instant control of the ball and the instinct to know when to pass, when to hold the ball and when to dribble, along with a subtle body swerve that could leave his marker totally stranded. No defender wanted to be embarrassed by such a performer.

One of the abiding memories of Celtic's famous 3–1 victory over Rangers in September 1948 was a moment in the second half when Tully received a pass near the halfway line. After gathering the ball neatly, Tully advanced a yard or two and almost visibly considered his options. Astonishingly, in the middle of this Old Firm clash – a match always played at a frenetic pace – not one member of Rangers' 'Iron Curtain' defence was willing to move to tackle the Celt. It would be tempting to embroider the story – to add that Tully waited for a few more seconds and then sat down on the ball (as Tommy McInally once did at a five-a-side tournament in the off-season) – but that would not be true. However, several Celtic supporters have stated since that they saw Charlie Tully do exactly that.

Johnny Paton, Tully's partner on Celtic's left wing during Tully's first season (1948–49), recalls that moment too: 'I have one particular memory of Charlie, and that was in the 3–1 win over Rangers in the League Cup in 1948. Charlie had possession in the middle of the park, and he stood there for several seconds as the whole Rangers defence stood mesmerised. Not too many players have that sort of ability: I think the last one was Jim Baxter playing for Scotland against England at Wembley.'

On occasion Tully used his quick-thinking to save himself. Sean Fallon smiles ruefully: 'You wouldn't want to have Charlie alongside you in a fight. He would be flattened with the first punch, or disappear.' Similarly, Willie Fernie recalls the visit to Rome in 1950, Celtic's only European trip during those seasons. The highlight was an audience with the Pope at St Peter's, but the tour included a friendly match against Lazio, arranged to mark the Italian club's 50th anniversary. The pitch was hard and firm, the weather a bit warm for Scottish tastes, and the contrast in playing styles occasionally caused friction on the pitch. Tully, in a mischievous mood, was guilty of a cheeky foul. Fernie remembers the event perfectly and has to smile at the recollection even half a century later. The opponent, typically Italian in appearance, looked a fearsome sight: 'Dark flashing eyes, unshaven, thick black hair, muscular and brown as a berry, he leapt to his feet and made towards Charlie with intent.' Tully found himself in a dilemma: he could have run away or stood his ground and hoped for help from his teammates before the enraged defender could reach him. The Italian made towards Tully with fists clenched and raised, and Tully reached out – the picture of innocence – to shake his hand.

His trick worked and defused that particular situation, although John McPhail and his immediate opponent were ordered off later after another altercation. Willie, a great admirer of Tully, also recalls that a return match was played later in the year at Celtic Park, and Celtic ran out comfortable winners by 4–0 before almost 50,000 at a rain-soaked Parkhead: 'Big John scored all four goals that night, two of them from penalty-kicks and the other two were headers from perfect crosses from Charlie Tully out on the left wing.'

Sean Fallon comments that 'Charlie had more years behind his ears than the rest of us' and cites an incident on the US tour in 1951 to back up his assertion. The players, although thrilled to be on such a tour, started to complain of the 'pocket money' they were getting. This was a traditional perk of overseas trips. Word reached chairman Bob Kelly about the complaints, and he set up court in the team's hotel near Times Square in New York. Bob Kelly sat at a table and called the players up one at a time. Tully was the first to go up to confront the chairman, while the others waited their turn downstairs. Thanks to some freak of acoustics, almost every word at the table could be heard downstairs. Fallon shakes his head at the memory.

Bob Kelly, as you would expect, went straight to the point: 'Are you one of those people looking for more money?' And I know for a fact that Charlie was afraid for his life of Bob Kelly and knew enough always to keep on the chairman's good side. Charlie was quick: 'No, not me, Mr Kelly. In fact, between ourselves, I think what we're getting is plenty. Our friends over here take us everywhere and pick up the bills. No, no we get enough, I assure you.' Every word could be heard, but when Charlie came down the staircase to rejoin us – while another player went up – he looked fiercely determined and growled: 'I bloody well told him!'

He may have been afraid of the chairman – the man who determined whether you stayed at Celtic Park or left, and who picked the team for the matches – but Tully was a skilled imitator of Bob Kelly's distinctive Lanarkshire rasping growl and amused the players at lunchtimes at Ferrari's Restaurant with the impersonations – and with thumping his right hand down on the table to emphasise a point as the chairman was wont to do. Almost needless to say, Kelly was never present at those times, but the impersonations always remained good natured with not a hint of cruelty or malice in them.

## Note

1. The referee that day was the highly respected George Mitchell (Falkirk), but he received a hostile reception at the end of the match, and one of his linesmen complained later that he had been spat upon by spectators. Police witnesses claimed not to have seen the incident and that the linesman had not mentioned this to them at the time. However, Mitchell was greeted coolly upon further visits to Celtic Park and never more so than on 20 August 1969 when, as the referee supervisor for an Old Firm League Cup tie, he was refused permission by an over-zealous doorman because he had forgotten his card. Accordingly, no referee supervisor was present on the night that the match official, Jim Callaghan, caused controversy by neglecting to order off John Hughes for an off-the-ball incident, on the say-so of his linesman. The referee was later suspended for six weeks by the SFA.

   The alleged misbehaviour in 1951 was also part of the SFA's case against Celtic in requesting that the club stop flying the Irish tricolour at Celtic Park.

# Chapter 9

## *Celtic's Achilles Heel*

This question has been asked often enough: why is it that Celtic, with such an array of talent on the books, were such consistent underachievers from the end of the war until 1965? Individuals such as Willie Miller, Pat McAuley, Bobby Evans, Bertie Peacock, Willie Fernie, Bobby Collins, Neil Mochan, John and Billy McPhail, Jimmy Walsh, John Higgins, Dick Beattie, Duncan MacKay and Charlie Tully, of course, were at Celtic Park among others during this period…but only one League title was won. The more observant would spot immediately that there is a shortage of first-class defenders on the list given and also that too many forwards were competing for the same berths. It made team selection problematic, and this was further complicated by the involvement of the chairman, Bob Kelly, in the process.

Jimmy McGrory, appointed in 1945, was simply an office manager and rarely appeared at training sessions, despite his legitimate claims to be one of Celtic's greatest-ever players. Billy McNeill, for one, is convinced that he did not own a tracksuit. Even worse was the fact that he had conceded control over team selection to the chairman. Not too surprisingly, his discipline was slack and several players took full advantage of that.

Bob Kelly was the ultimate authority, but he was very removed from the one-to-one give-and-take of the factory floor. Sometimes, he had an idealistic view of the reality of the modern professional game, and he could be hoodwinked by certain players. Bob Crampsey has stated 'Bob Kelly's ideal Celtic team would be decent young lads, straight out of Boys' Guild teams, all with great natural ability, all playing attacking football – and willing to play for Celtic for nothing.'

Blind to glaring deficiencies in some areas, Kelly could be draconian in his treatment of those who had offended his code of values. Some players, for offences on the field, fell out of favour and were punished. Bobby Collins was dropped from the Scottish Cup Final replay against Clyde in 1955 after being involved in an undignified dunting match with Clyde's 'keeper Ken Hewkins. Hewkins was well over 6ft and Collins was officially listed at 5ft 3in, but Kelly felt that Celtic's code of conduct had been breached. A year later, when preparing for the Cup Final against Hearts, Jim Sharkey was involved in a minor incident at the team's hotel, and Kelly was informed. His reaction was to drop Sharkey, but this meant wholesale changes in Celtic's line up in almost every department. Not too surprisingly, both of those Scottish Cup Finals were lost. Sean Fallon, although a great admirer of the chairman, has to admit 'If Bob Kelly didn't like you, then you were on your way pretty quickly.'

Such maladministration could only lead to cliques within the squad, and Charlie Tully could be considered a willing participator. Every group of players has a natural leader or a number of leaders, but unfortunately this is not confined to the playing field. When Tully arrived from Belfast in 1948, Celtic had no recognised team leader on the pitch – but they had some in off-field antics, not particularly vicious ones but the harmless excesses that most young men can find themselves involved in. But these were not the average young men; they were, or were supposed to be, athletes in training.

Most of those familiar with the time at Celtic Park would identify Jock Weir and John McPhail as Charlie Tully's cronies in his early days in Glasgow. Tully, acknowledged as an up-and-coming star player, was vulnerable: in a strange city, ill-at-ease with his surroundings, cut off from his tightly knit community in Belfast, adjusting to a new team and training methods and also a very sociable man, who delighted in company. It was no surprise that he should fall in with Weir and McPhail.

Jock Weir had been signed by Celtic from Blackburn Rovers for £7,000 in a successful bid to escape from relegation. In fact he was credited – wrongly – for having 'saved' Celtic with his hat-trick against Dundee on the last day of the 1947–48 season, and his status as 'a Celtic hero' was confirmed. Either as centre-forward or outside-right, he was a limited player. He had speed, strength and enthusiasm but lacked ball-control and composure. A few weeks before his heroics at Dens Park, he had missed the most glaring of chances to put Celtic ahead in extra-time of the Scottish Cup semi-final against Morton; from only a couple of yards out, he stabbed the ball past Jimmy Cowan's post.

He had been around, had Jock Weir. During the war he served in the Fleet Air Arm and had played for Hibernian, Cardiff City and Brighton & Hove Albion before joining Blackburn Rovers. Charlie Tully himself relates that Jock Weir was installed by Celtic in the Kenilworth Hotel (at the corner of Queen Street and Argyle Street) while he was being repatriated; admiringly, Tully reports that Weir was still living rent-free in the hotel 18 months later! Not too surprisingly, after his retirement as a player Jock Weir ended up . as the manager of a public house.

John McPhail, on the other hand, was a one-club player. Signed from St Mungo's Academy (and Strathclyde Juniors) in 1941, he was still on Celtic's books until 1956. Unlike Weir, he was a talented player, and throughout a lengthy career at Parkhead he turned out for Celtic in eight different positions, despite the fact that he remained exclusively and stubbornly right-footed. McPhail was always a popular figure with the Celtic supporters because they identified with him: a Glasgow boy, a Catholic school, a Celtic supporter and a great player who never realised his full potential. He may have been unlucky with an outbreak of tuberculosis that sidelined him for most of 1946 and 1947, but his later weight problems should have been identified more quickly and remedied. But John, secure in his position at Celtic Park (mainly as a result of the 1951 Scottish Cup triumph), was not inclined to train too strenuously. He and Charlie Tully had formed a formidable partnership on the field, with many of McPhail's goals coming from headers after pin-point crosses from Tully. Off-field (along with Jock Weir), they were constant companions. Billy Tully puts it bluntly: 'Jock Weir and John McPhail didn't help Charlie. My brother didn't drink very much until he met them. They led him astray – but, mind you, Charlie probably didn't need too much leading.'

Audrey Douglas (who later married Willie Fernie) was Jimmy McGrory's secretary and close to the players, as they trained at Celtic Park daily. Some were in and out of her office for all sorts of help. For example, she was responsible for arranging John McPhail's honeymoon with his wife Ella in Jersey. She agrees that John McPhail, Jock Weir and Charlie Tully were 'buddies' on and off the pitch and suspects that they may have spent too much of their spare time drinking together. She thinks that Jock Weir was the most 'gallus' of the three and probably the most worldly. She confirms the story of his prolonged stay at the Kenilworth Hotel at Celtic's expense. Audrey remembers Charlie Tully as 'a most pleasant young man, and a great personality. He was always particular in his language towards me and any other women in and around the club. A lovely man, a gentleman'.

After retiring and making way for his younger brother, Billy, to join Celtic from Clyde, John McPhail worked as a journalist – first with the *Daily Record* and latterly with the *Celtic View*. Reportedly, he did not take his duties too seriously. It was rumoured that he sent in some match reports to the *Daily Record* from a pub adjacent to the ground where he was supposed to be working.

Unfortunately, such cliques within a football club can lead to consequences on the pitch. It appears clear that some players, newcomers to Celtic, were not made welcome and departed quickly without being given a true chance to make a contribution to the club.

Leslie Johnston was bought from Clyde on 28 October 1948 for £12,000, a clear indication that the Celtic directors recognised the need for a proven goalscorer. Johnston, a much-travelled player in the late 1940s (Clyde–Hibernian–Clyde–Celtic–Stoke City within two years), made an excellent start to his Celtic career by scoring both goals in a 2–1 win over Hibernian at Easter Road on 30 October, only four days after his capture. However, he never looked entirely at ease within Celtic Park, fluctuating among the three inside-forward positions. Certainly, he did not appear on the same wavelength as his colleagues, and I have a distinct recollection of a 0–0 match on a heavy pitch at Cappielow on 8 January 1949. Celtic were pressing in the second half and a long pass from Evans reached Johnston. It would have been a difficult ball to control, but Johnston cleverly touched the ball down the left wing – a delicate glance that deceived the defence. It was a touch that should have been seized upon by an alert winger, but Tully ignored the ball and made no effort to collect it. From some vantage points on the terracing, it looked as if Leslie Johnston had actually missed the ball altogether (and Tully's lack of effort to chase it furthered that impression). Predictably, the Celtic followers hurled abuse at the guiltless Johnston but he glared over at Tully, who ignored the look.

Had Charlie Tully been caught by surprise by Johnston's flick, or was he prepared to let a fellow professional take the blame – mainly because he did not fit in with the reigning clique on the pitch at Celtic Park? Whatever, I – for one – was not too surprised when Celtic were turfed out of the Scottish Cup 4–3 by lower-division Dundee United at Tannadice, two weeks later.

Gil Heron was another victim of the cliques operating within Celtic Park. The Jamaican-born centre-forward had been discovered on Celtic's tour of the United States in 1951, having impressed against Celtic in Detroit. He was a tall, rangy forward with a fine turn of speed and a blistering shot, but his career at Parkhead was short. He made his debut[1] against Morton in a League Cup sectional game and scored Celtic's second goal with a 20-yard shot against their international 'keeper Jimmy Cowan. Heron continued with another appearance in the same competition against Third Lanark in a 1–0 win at Cathkin.

He also featured against Airdrie in a 2–0 win at Celtic Park and scored a spectacular goal past Fraser (later another Scottish international goalkeeper) from 25 yards, and he played in a 2–0 loss to Morton at Cappielow. His four appearances in the League Cup had produced two goals for him, and Celtic's qualification for the later stages of the competition. However, with the restoration of John McPhail to Celtic's first XI, Gil Heron was demoted to the reserves and played in only one further match (a 2–1 win over Partick Thistle on 1 December 1951).

A Glasgow Cup tie against Third Lanark on 3 September 1951 was significant in that it revealed the attitude of some Celtic players. John McPhail had returned from the American tour considerably overweight and out of shape. Celtic had persevered with him in the early stages of the St Mungo Cup, but he was eventually replaced by Sean Fallon and later Gil Heron. McPhail was restored for this Cup tie (won 5–2 by Celtic at Cathkin Park) but did not appear fully fit and was certainly far from mobile. Celtic played very well in the opening stages, but play broke down several times when the ball was in the vicinity of McPhail. On one occasion, a frustrated Bobby Collins – in an exaggerated manner – passed the ball straight to John McPhail rather than in front of him, as if to point out that the centre-forward was not quick enough to move very far to collect the ball.

Football teams are always in some stage of transition. A team needs veteran players as well as youngsters, experience as well as enthusiasm and newcomers to freshen up a stale squad, but an incomer represents a threat to the regulars and is not always welcomed. That is when a manager has to be strong-willed, but Jimmy McGrory was never that type. Accordingly, Gil Heron and Leslie Johnston before him – goalscorers who could have made a real difference to Celtic's fortunes on the field – were frozen out in preference to more established players.

Charlie Tully was an exception because, almost immediately upon his arrival at Celtic Park, he had made such an impression that he became indispensable. Nobody could question the fact that he had instigated a considerable improvement, and it helped that the man he replaced (Gerry McAloon) had gone to Belfast Celtic later in a form of exchange.

Even worse was the uneasy suspicion that some games were 'fixed', and the finger kept pointing in the direction of 'keeper Dick Beattie. Later in his career in England (January 1965), Beattie was jailed for nine months for 'throwing games', and a furious Derek Dougan once almost attacked him at Peterborough United after a very suspect goal. In this light, a couple of Celtic games might be recalled and re-examined: the Scottish Cup semi-final replay against Kilmarnock in 1957 was an obvious example, with Beattie's eccentricities arousing widespread comment, and the Scottish Cup Final against Hearts in 1956 might also be cited. John Bonnar, who had been replaced by Beattie as Celtic's first-string goalkeeper, told a contributor to *The Celt* that he felt two of the three goals given up by Beattie that day could have been stopped, although he did not suggest outright any deliberate action by the 'keeper.

In a similar way, Celtic's veteran centre-half Bobby Evans was becoming implicated. The relationship between a centre-half and his goalkeeper is a delicate one, depending often on split-second decision-making and trust, but frequently that season goals were being given up due to 'misunderstandings' between Evans and Beattie. This was highly unusual for a pivot of Evans's experience, but it still came as a major shock when he was transferred to Chelsea in 1960 at very short notice. Unfortunately, suspicion followed him to London, and his stay with Chelsea proved short – a sad ending to a glittering career after so many seasons of impeccable service to Celtic.

It gives me no pleasure to write about these suspicions, and for many years I had assumed that any mistakes on Evans's part were due to the bounce of the ball or errors in concentration to be expected of a player past his best. I am no longer sure. Fixed-odds betting had an appeal for players in the know and prepared to cheat in order to make money. This was clearly the case with Beattie, but Bobby Evans…?

Whether any Celtic player ever intentionally 'threw' a game is irrelevant in a biography of Charlie Tully, but the fact that the issue could be raised at all is an indication of a malaise within the club. Nobody seemed to be in a position of 'hands-on' control: McGrory was ineffectual, Kelly was too remote (and probably too idealistic to consider the possibility) and the trainers had little say. The situation cried out for a strong figure to take charge, but Jock Stein's appointment was almost a decade away in the future. A strong-willed manager would have sorted that situation out immediately, but McGrory could not. Similarly, such a manager would never have tolerated any cliques within the club (or team) that affected performance on the pitch.

How would Celtic (and Charlie Tully) have done with a strong manager? Perhaps a manager as single-minded as Jock Stein would not have been the best for a player like Tully. Jimmy Farrell, the former Celtic director, told me:

*Jock Stein was no admirer of Charlie Tully. He resented his attitude towards training and his attempts to get out of it. He felt that it was a neglect of a great talent — and basically unprofessional. Stein, of course — as an average player himself — had to work hard to keep his place in the team. As a defender, he could be critical of Tully's reluctance to double back and help out when required. As a manager, he would never have considered Charlie Tully as a player, mainly because of his individualism and attitude; it would have interfered with the idea of teamwork.*

Would Charles Patrick Tully have changed his ways? In fact, could he? It should always be remembered that Charlie Tully, appearances to the contrary, loved the game itself and was a keen student of it. He lived for and loved the thrill of performing. Given that, and knowing that his future as a player might depend on a more professional attitude and commitment, it is inconceivable that he would not have responded favourably – and much to the benefit of both player and club.

## Note

1. Celtic were not above promoting this debut, with newspapers tipped off about the newcomer already nicknamed 'The Black Flash'. Black players were a rarity in Britain at this time. In fact, I was present at that match, sheltering from the heavy rain in 'The Jungle' and, when the teams appeared for the kick-in just prior to the match, several youngsters raced on to the pitch for Heron's autograph. To considerable amusement, they made straight for Jimmy Mallan, whose deep tan appeared several shades darker than Heron's. Those interested in music might know that his son is the well-known jazz artist Gil Scott Heron.

# Chapter 10

## — *A Luxury Player?* —

A frequent criticism made of entertaining players is that they do not work hard enough and that, despite their undoubted skill, they represent a luxury that teams cannot afford. In the modern game, with the emphasis on work rate and athleticism, a player exhibiting only skill is indeed a luxury, and effectiveness has to be considered.

Charlie Tully was a case in point. Some teammates, including his captain Jock Stein, could be scathing about Tully's reluctance to help out in defence and his chronic inability to tackle opponents. Speaking as a manager, Stein remained adamant that the Irishman would not have featured in his teams unless he had mended his ways. It is a valid criticism, but Sean Fallon, just as earnest and serious about football as Stein, remembers Tully as a valuable outlet: 'I can remember Charlie drifting back into our penalty area and telling us "If you're getting tired, give the ball to me and I'll give you a rest."'

An analogy from American football might illustrate the situation: the most valuable player in the team is the quarterback, the man who makes all the decisions on the offense. Sometimes, a fumble or an interception takes place and the ball is recovered by the opposing team. NFL coaches age prematurely at the thought of their quarterback attempting to tackle in an attempt to halt the turnover; that is the primary responsibility of less talented, more expendable players. In this case, it is the possibility of injury to such a valuable member of the team that worries the coaching staff. What would the point be of a Charlie Tully – or a Lubomir Moravcik – exhausting himself by helping out in defence to such an extent that he cannot take full advantage of attacking opportunities at the other end of the pitch? How does the football man evaluate the effectiveness of a player such as Charlie Tully? One form of 'evidence' might be to compare his seasons at Celtic Park with how his club were doing prior to his arrival and how they did after his departure.

Celtic may have been one of the most famous football clubs in the world, but it was an organisation in decline in 1948, the year of Tully's arrival. Consider the evidence: the last triumph in the Scottish Cup had taken place in 1937; the last League Championship had been won in 1938; the last League and Cup double had been accomplished in 1914; and 'the greatest cup-fighting team in Scotland' had made no impression at all in the early years of the League Cup competition. This was hardly a football club at the height of its powers. However, Charlie Tully made a difference, not single-handedly, admittedly, but he was one of the principal architects of Celtic's revival in the 1950s.

The results are interesting to say the least. During Tully's time as a Celtic player (from his arrival in 1948 to his departure in 1959), the club's list of honours read as follows: one League Championship (1953–54), two Scottish Cups (1951 and 1954), two League Cups (1956 and 1957), two Glasgow Cups (1948 and 1955), three Glasgow Charity Cups (1950, 1953 and 1959), a Coronation Cup (1953) and a St Mungo Cup (1951). Cynics might consider – and reasonably so – that the overall record should have been much better given the calibre of players such as Tully, Evans, Peacock, Collins and Fernie. However, it was a time of genuine competition, with several clubs competing seriously for the prizes.

Later, Jock Stein claimed that during this period a reasonable division of the spoils (the League Championship, the Scottish Cup and the League Cup) would have been Rangers and Celtic each winning one major trophy and the rest picking up the other every season. After this unofficial table of 33 competitions was completed, the reasonable outcome (according to Jock Stein's logic) would have been as follows: Rangers (11), Celtic (11) and Others (11). Presumably, Stein – as a practical man – was thinking of the massive advantage the Old Firm clubs hold in finances and in support – factors which should have produced such results. However, that was not the case, as this table indicating trophy wins between 1948 and 1959 (Charlie's time at Celtic Park) clearly shows:

| League Championship: | Rangers 6 | Celtic 1 | Others 4 |
| --- | --- | --- | --- |
| Scottish Cup: | Rangers 3 | Celtic 2 | Others 6 |
| League Cup: | Rangers 1 | Celtic 2 | Others 8 |

In this golden age of true competition, the League Championship was won by Hibernian (2), Aberdeen (1) and Hearts (1); the Scottish Cup was won by Clyde (2), Motherwell (1), Hearts (1), Falkirk (1) and St Mirren (1); and the League Cup was won by East Fife (2), Dundee (2), Hearts (2), Motherwell (1) and Aberdeen (1). The overall results were as follows: Rangers (10), Celtic (5), Others (16). Rangers came close to meeting Stein's 'target' and, as the Championship is recognised as the truest test of a football team, perhaps they should be given the credit for attaining it. Celtic, on the other hand, 'failed' with only half of Rangers' trophy total. The surprise might lie in the number of competitions won by the other clubs. The individual total for these 'Others' was as follows: Hearts (4), Hibernian (2), Aberdeen (2), Motherwell (2), East Fife (2), Dundee (2), Falkirk (1), St Mirren (1).

If competition is the key to enthralling football, then the 'Tully Years' were a Golden Age for Scottish football – but sadly Celtic, for a number of reasons (mostly self-inflicted), fell well short. As a digression, it could be pointed out that Celtic were poorly served in one aspect of organisation – a leader in central defence.

Belfast Celtic's Jackie Vernon – a life-long friend of Charlie Tully's – was a commanding, no-nonsense centre-half, and Glasgow Celtic were interested in him in late 1946. Vernon was ready to move to Glasgow, but the Parkhead club felt the valuation of £8,000 was too high. In February 1947 he was transferred for £9,500 to West Bromwich Albion, where he played for five seasons. It should be pointed out that others had an equally high opinion of Vernon as a stopper centre-half: he played for Great

Britain against the Rest of the World at Hampden Park in 1947, in preference to such players as Willie Woodburn (Scotland) and Neil Franklin (England).

During the time of Vernon's career, Celtic fielded centre-halves such as Jimmy Mallan, John McGrory, Alec Boden, Willie Corbett and Duncan McMillan – none of whom was in the same class as Vernon. It was not until the veteran journeyman Jock Stein was signed from Llanelly in 1951 that Celtic acquired a centre-half capable of organising a defence. Vernon had the authority and the presence to do that – and certainly Celtic's results would have been much better.

Another recurring complaint of Celtic supporters (and it was a legitimate one) is that Celtic never seemed to be capable of fielding a settled forward line. Hibernian had their 'Famous Five' of Smith, Johnstone, Reilly, Turnbull and Ormond, while Hearts had their 'Terrible Trio' of Conn, Bauld and Wardhaugh, but nobody could predict confidently what Celtic's latest forward permutation would be. Tully was fielded in every forward position except centre-forward, as was Bobby Collins. John McPhail, Willie Fernie and Jimmy Walsh also played in four of the five traditional forward positions, while Neil Mochan flitted between centre-forward and outside-left – and this makes no mention of the numerous 'short-term wonders' who briefly flared into prominence and then faded into obscurity. The culprit in this matter was the chairman, who took it upon himself to meddle with team selection, often with horrific results.[1] Older supporters will recall the bizarre forward permutations in successive Scottish Cup Finals – both, of course, lost – against Clyde and Hearts in the mid-1950s.

Football restarted in a manner for the 1945–46 season, although this was declared an 'unofficial' transitional campaign. Celtic played three post-war seasons before Tully arrived at Celtic Park, so from the point of view of symmetry, the three seasons after his return to Ireland have been selected for comparison.

Between 1945–46 and 1947–48, Rangers won exactly half of the competitions, while Aberdeen, East Fife and Hibernian picked up the others. Even in the less important competitions, such as the Glasgow Cup and Charity Cup, Rangers dominated with four successes, the other two going to Queen's Park and Clyde.

Celtic, whose performance level and application throughout the wartime seasons had been shameful for a club of its standing, had continued the downward spiral in the early peacetime seasons. In the first place, they did not win a trophy, major or minor, in the 12 opportunities afforded to them. Their poor record in the League Championship – and in those seasons when only two points were awarded for a win – shows the slide downwards to the edge of the relegation zone:

|  | P | W | D | L | F – A | Pts | Position |
|---|---|---|---|---|---|---|---|
| 1945–46 | 30 | 12 | 11 | 7 | 55 – 44 | 35 | 4th |
| 1946–47 | 30 | 13 | 6 | 11 | 53 – 55 | 32 | 7th |
| 1947–48 | 30 | 10 | 5 | 15 | 41 – 56 | 25 | 12th |

It was only in the aftermath of the indignity of having to go to Dens Park on Celtic's last match of the 1947–48 season and having to win to banish any threat of relegation that Celtic made a move for Charlie Tully.

Let us turn to the three seasons following his retirement as a Celtic player and consider the club's level of attainment (again using Jock Stein's system of evaluation):

*League Championship: Rangers 1  Celtic 0  Others 2 (Hearts 1, Dundee 1)*

*Scottish Cup:        Rangers 2  Celtic 0  Others 1 (Dunfermline 1)*

*League Cup:          Rangers 2  Celtic 0  Others 1 (Hearts 1)*

The logical conclusion to be drawn is that Celtic did reach a level of respectability during the seasons Charlie Tully played for the club, but not the standard expected and nowadays demanded. We can see that in the three seasons preceding Tully's transfer from Belfast Celtic, the Glasgow club won exactly nothing – and indeed were living dangerously. In the three seasons after his departure, once more Celtic won nothing, although they had at least risen to a level of mediocrity and occasionally gave some indications of breaking through into the top flight.

An even more damning picture could have been presented by extending this period to 1964–65, when Billy McNeill's late winner against Dunfermline Athletic ended 'seven lean years' – perhaps the most frustrating period in the club's history.

The apologist for Charlie Tully could claim that he had made a difference, clearly obvious even in the bare statistics. This indicates that Tully, although sometimes considered only a 'luxury' by some, contributed considerably to the club's success on the pitch. And it could be argued equally convincingly that Charlie Tully revitalised the shaky finances of the club. Certainly, Tully's arrival in 1948 had an immediate impact on attendances.[2]

The sectional play in the League Cup always took place early in the season. Those six games and the League fixtures that took place in conjunction with them have been examined from 1947–48, 1948–49, 1958–59 and 1959–60 – the season before Tully arrived, his first season, his last season and the season after his departure.

In 1947–48 Celtic played eight games (against Rangers, Dundee and Third Lanark, home and away, and against Queen's Park and Airdrie in the League). The average home attendance was 31,333, and the away average was 38,750.

In 1948–49 (Charlie Tully's first season), Celtic played 12 games in a similar period (against Rangers, Hibernian and Clyde, home and away, and against Morton, Rangers,

Aberdeen, Hearts, Queen of the South and Albion Rovers in the League). The average home attendance was 49,178, and the away average was 47,333.

In 1958–59 (Charlie Tully's last season) Celtic played only six relevant matches as the season opened with the League Cup section of Clyde, Airdrie and St Mirren. Their average attendance at home was 39,000, and the away average was 20,500.

In 1959–60 seven matches can be considered (against Partick Thistle, Raith Rovers and Airdrie, home and away, and Kilmarnock in the League). The average attendance at home was 24,500 and 17,333 away.

This is not a perfect comparison, but the basic fact remains unchallenged that in the opening games during Charlie Tully's first season with Celtic, the overall average attendance, home and away, was an astonishing 48,256. For the previous season, the average for similar fixtures was 35,000. In the season following his departure, the average attendance slumped to 20,916, down from an average of 25,125 in his last season.

A strong case could be made that Charlie Tully, apart from what he did as a footballer, revitalised Celtic's finances. Certainly, he repaid his transfer fee if only by increased revenue at the turnstiles – and this makes no comment on his contribution as a player in helping Celtic to the Finals of major competitions, and the greater interest and crowds this generated.

Fortunately, though, football is not a matter of statistics. For the enthusiast, it gives unalloyed pleasure in appreciation of the imagination employed in creating goalscoring opportunities with an incisive pass or perfectly placed cross, and the control and courage shown in taking on defenders and dribbling past them. Add to this the extra pleasure given by a natural entertainer who plays with a smile on his face, and you are getting closer to the image of Charlie Tully. One more ingredient helps complete the picture: the idea of a personality who transforms events, changing the reality of a situation for the better, and a man who inspires and provides hope or optimism for a desperate multitude. And all this with talent, skill and humour.

As the journalist (and long-time Celtic observer) Hugh Keevins points out 'It is not by ability alone that a Celtic player becomes revered in the eyes of the support or has his memory cherished long after his days with the club are at an end. Talent is the basis on which adoration is earned but to be possessed of other attributes that impinge the individual on the consciousness of the faithful is to be admitted to the select few who have had legendary status bestowed upon them at Celtic Park.'

And this brings us to the question of how Charlie Tully would do in the modern game. First of all, he did quite well against the players of his own time. As a winger, he faced up to truly terrifying full-backs like Emery and Lapsley. In fairness it should be noted that Don Emery (Aberdeen) and Dave Lapsley (St Mirren), while physically imposing, were sporting opponents and used their strength in the tackle within the framework of the rules, which, during Tully's career, did allow a measure of physicality. He matched wits with the scrupulously clean, like George Young and Alf Ramsey. As an inside-forward, he was not found wanting in clashes with Ian McColl (Rangers), Dave MacKay (Hearts), Joe Mercer (Arsenal) and Billy Wright (Wolverhampton Wanderers). Playing for Northern Ireland he found himself on the same pitch as Stanley Matthews, Tom Finney, Alfredo Di Stefano, Ladislav Kubala, Raymond Kopa and Francisco Gento, and he was not out of place in that exalted company.

How would Jack Nicklaus or Tom Watson do on the present-day PGA Golf Tour if they had the advantage of modern technology? Or how would Bobby Jones do? The answer is obvious: a sportsman (whether a golfer or footballer) will rise to the top if he has the innate ability and the will to do so. Charlie Tully would never have lost that enthusiasm. Thus, he would have wanted to play, and the opportunity would have been presented to him, given his talent.

When Tully played in Belfast and Glasgow, athleticism was not the mark of a footballer as it is now. He was never a great trainer, nor did he take particularly good care of himself, but he did not flag unduly in the closing stages of hard-fought matches. Johnny Paton describes his physical attributes: 'He was a natural athlete, slimly built and flexible, very well balanced. He didn't have to train hard to watch his weight as, say, bigger players like John McPhail or Jackie Gallagher.' Sean Fallon claims tolerantly there was little resentment about Tully's work rate and reluctance to help out in defence, adding with a smile 'He would have just got in the way.' Billy McNeill, while admitting Tully's aversion to the physical grind of training, points out 'Celtic had some super-fit players around him who could compensate; Bobby Evans, Bobby Collins, Willie Fernie and Bertie Peacock trained like demons and could help Charlie out sometimes on the Saturday.'

Charlie Tully, behind the mask of entertainer, was a highly competitive individual. He was naturally fit, and he felt that was enough. On the field, responding to the occasion and the expectation of the crowd willing him on, he could rely on a surge of adrenaline and the sense of excitement to get him through the hardest of matches. In this respect, he was very similar to Paul Gascoigne during his Rangers days.

There have been perhaps only five occasions when a player, a manager or an event has made an impact on Celtic and effected a sea change in the club's fortunes. These occasions were the dramatic appearance of the club on the football scene in 1888, the arrival of Jock Stein as Celtic's manager in 1965, the emergence of Fergus McCann as a financial saviour in 1994, the appointment of Martin O'Neill as Celtic's manager in 2000 and, comparable to these milestones, the signing and arrival in Glasgow of Charles Patrick Tully from Belfast Celtic in 1948.

But how would Charlie Tully do in modern football? Well if he were available today and starting off in his career, he would still have his talent, described by Sean Fallon as 'a wonderful touch on the ball, a genius with the ball'. He would still have that ability to improvise, to do the unexpected and destroy defences with one move, and he would still possess the confidence in himself to exploit his own gifts to the full but, aware of the salaries available for today's stars, he would have made himself a fitter player and a better team player. He may not have had a great head for (or interest in) finance, but offered the prospect of earning thousands of pounds a week, it is impossible to believe that he would not have prepared to ready himself for the demanding schedule of the modern game. But would he have been fast enough? Probably not, but as Sean Fallon points out emphatically 'Charlie was lightning-fast between his ears – and no player can move faster than the ball.'

Patsy's son Tommy Gallacher, after a distinguished career with Queen's Park and Dundee, became a journalist in Dundee. 'What he lacked in pace and strength, Charlie made up in other ways, like taking the ball right up to the full-back and showing that he was a masterful dribbler,' he says. 'No player gets that much praise for so long unless he is doing something to deserve it.'

The fact is that given his sublime skills and ones sharpened by greater fitness, Charlie Tully would be employed by a thoughtful coach as a midfield player – and not as a ball-winner but as a creative playmaker. He would be capable of winning any match with one devastating manoeuvre, or controlling the pace of the game by adroit possession play. Tully would have been a quarterback (American-style).

## Notes

1. One example might suffice. In 1955 Celtic went to Ibrox in the League Cup and won convincingly by 4–1. The return was at Celtic Park four days later. Willie Fernie had been injured at Ibrox but after treatment he reported to Celtic Park fully prepared to play. Bob Kelly told him 'Don't worry, Willie. We can win this game easily enough without you.' A youngster called Matt McVittie was chosen in Fernie's place, and Celtic lost 4–0 – their largest-ever margin of defeat in a League Cup game at Celtic Park.

2. Celtic were notoriously reluctant to reveal actual attendances, and most of the figures used are intelligent estimates. Charlie Tully did play in the vast majority of these games, and all the matches were played at the start of the season when expectations are highest. In 1947–48 and 1948–49 the schedule contained fixtures against Rangers, and these large attendances would distort the averages somewhat. In all of the seasons, League matches were played prior to the start of the League Cup, and these have been included in the figures.

# Chapter 11

# One-offs

Charlie Tully has frequently been described as 'a one-off'. Accordingly, it is highly appropriate that he should have played a leading role in two such competitions won by Celtic in the early 1950s.

The Festival of Britain took place throughout 1951, and Glasgow Corporation contributed by staging a football competition, run along knock-out lines in the summer. Celtic, as the holders of the Scottish Cup, were among the favourites to win. Also, they had just returned from a tour of the United States and presumably were in better shape than most of their opponents.

The first round was staged on 14 July, the Saturday of the Glasgow Fair, and the weather was brilliant throughout Scotland that day. Celtic, entertaining Hearts at Celtic Park before a shirt-sleeved crowd of 51,000, entered the field to a rapturous reception and outplayed the Edinburgh visitors to win 2–1.

The second round, for some strange reason, was played on neutral ground, and Celtic faced Clyde at Firhill. Partick Thistle's ground had a reputation for staging thrilling matches, and this was one of the epic struggles there. Clyde, recently relegated to Division B, somehow endured Celtic's opening burst of pressure and led 2–0 after 15 minutes, both goals scored by Alec Linwood. Celtic fought back and were level shortly after the interval. The assumption was that Celtic would go on to win comfortably, but with only eight minutes left in the Cup tie, Clyde were leading by 4–2, and Celtic were on the verge of elimination. John McPhail, clearly overweight upon his return from America, headed in a cross from Joe Baillie and injured Clyde's 'keeper, Miller, in the process. He required lengthy treatment from the trainer, and Celtic intensified the pressure when the 'keeper elected to play on, although obviously dazed. Bobby Collins equalised in the last minute, shooting for goal through a crowded goalmouth to let Celtic escape.

Celtic, with Sean Fallon at centre-forward, won the replay easily by 4–1 and faced Raith Rovers at Hampden Park in the semi-final. Celtic won the match 3–1 with Jimmy Walsh, a new signing from Bo'ness United, scoring all three, but he was not Celtic's star. That was Charlie Tully on the left wing, facing one of his regular victims – the full-back McClure, whom he had tormented in the previous Scottish Cup semi-final. And he did it again, beating the defender in every possible way, spreading panic throughout the Rovers defence – and thoroughly enjoying himself.

The Final, against Aberdeen on 1 August 1951 at Hampden Park, attracted a crowd of 81,000. The line up was as follows:

**Aberdeen:** Martin, Emery, Shaw, Harris, Thomson, Lowrie, Bogan, Yorston, Hamilton, Baird, Hather.

**Celtic:** Hunter, Haughney, Rollo, Evans, Mallan, Baillie, Collins, Walsh, Fallon, Peacock, Tully.

Aberdeen were first to settle and put Celtic on the defensive with bright, attractive play, which stretched Celtic's defence. At 14 minutes, Aberdeen took the lead when Yorston hooked the ball into the Celtic net past George Hunter, who had collided with a post and hurt himself. While the 'keeper was off for treatment, Bobby Evans took his place and showed his relief when the Celtic goalkeeper returned with his head heavily bandaged; Evans raced out of the goal like a scalded cat. Aberdeen, although pushed back into defence, broke away and scored a second goal at 35 minutes. For the third time in the St Mungo Cup[1], Celtic found themselves two goals down.

Charlie Tully led the anticipated Celtic revival. He had started to wander in search of the ball and found himself on the right wing jousting with David Shaw, Aberdeen's left-back. Tully won a throw-in near the corner flag and, as the defender trotted away into position, Tully played the ball off his retreating back. And the referee (J.A. Mowat) awarded Celtic a corner-kick. Shaw was upset at the decision and protested at length, but Mr Mowat saw nothing wrong with Tully's action. Almost inevitably in the case of Charlie Tully, the incident was not over. An upset Aberdeen defence failed to clear his corner properly, and Sean Fallon scrambled the ball in, with only one minute left in the first half.

Celtic took over in the second half. Charlie Tully, now back on his usual left-wing beat and faced with the redoubtable Don Emery, was visibly lifted by the success of his first-half gambit. He started to hold the ball and torment the defender. Early in the second half, Sean Fallon equalised with a fine goal, gathering the ball from combined play on the left. And Celtic's winning goal, inevitable by that stage, was engineered by Tully. He gathered the pass from Baillie, slipped past Emery yet again, passed to Peacock and caught the return pass on the byline, before crossing for Walsh to score. And once again there was some controversy, as the Aberdeen defenders claimed that the ball had crossed the byline before Tully caught it.

A 'one-off' competition won mainly through the skill of a 'one-off' player! It may have been described as one-off but the trophy, while handsome in appearance, turned out to have a somewhat tarnished pedigree. It proved to be second-hand, having been crafted in 1894 for a yachting competition, and had re-emerged in

1912 when it was presented to Provan Gas Works after they beat Glasgow Police (at least in football).

* * *

The Coronation Cup of 1953 was Scotland's contribution to the celebrations as Queen Elizabeth II ascended the throne. It was to be an invitational tournament with four teams from Scotland (Rangers, Aberdeen, Hibernian and Celtic) and four from England (Arsenal, Tottenham Hotspur, Manchester United and Newcastle United).

With the exception of Celtic, all the sides merited inclusion in such a prestigious competition: Celtic had won nothing that season and were struggling in the League, and several newspapers made the pointed suggestion that Celtic withdraw to avoid humiliation. Merit would not be the only pre-requisite for inclusion,[2] as 50 per cent of the revenue from the competition was to go to charities, and the organisers felt that Celtic's participation would produce one healthy first-round 'gate' and an early exit, widely predicted after the draw pitted them against the English champions, Arsenal. The line up was as follows:

**Arsenal:** Swindon, Wade, Chentall, Forbes, Dodgin, Mercer, Roper, Goring, Holton, Lishman, Marden.

**Celtic:** Bonnar, Haughney, Rollo, Evans, Stein, McPhail, Collins, Walsh, Mochan, Peacock, Tully.

Arsenal casually dominated the proceedings for the first five minutes, moving the ball from man to man and denying Celtic possession. Bobby Evans acted decisively to halt this. Stepping in to break up another Arsenal raid, he intercepted a slightly errant pass, rounded an opponent and sent a searching ball forward for Walsh, whose flashing shot grazed the post. And the crowd realised immediately that the Englishmen had been caught flat-footed and were not a football team from another planet.

Similarly, Charlie Tully was not the sort of player to accept watching another team dominating possession. More and more, Celtic came into the match; and more and more, Tully prompted his forwards. Bobby Collins took a leaf from Tully's guide to taking corner-kicks, and his flag-kick deceived George Swindon in the 21st minute. Arsenal's veteran 'keeper made up for his lapse as Celtic continued to attack, and he astonishingly had to save at the feet of Celtic's left-back, Rollo – and remember that backs in the 1950s seldom strayed into enemy territory.

Celtic's display was a revelation for those who had seen them struggling for months, and remarkably it came in the wake of a short-lived player revolt. The 'regulations' for the tournament, drawn up by a semi-feudal SFA, decreed that the players of all clubs would receive £10 per game – and this was for football matches played in May, traditionally the closed season. Both the English and Scottish Players' Unions petitioned the football authorities and the Ministry of Labour for better conditions – and, considering that the attendance for the eight Cup ties came to 440,526, they certainly had a case.[3]

Bob Kelly had heard of the player dissatisfaction and, typically, dealt with it face-to-face with the Celtic players individually. He made it clear that his only concern was the willingness of each player to play in the competition and refused to discuss any question of a bonus. The players agreed, perhaps reluctantly, and the matter, at least at Celtic Park, was resolved.

Several years later, a story surfaced regarding the payment to the players. As the organising committee was meeting on the morning of the Final, a communication was received from Celtic Park. It contained the assertion that the Coronation Cup Final would not be played unless changes were made to the amount of remuneration owed to the players. Needless to say, the Final was played, and the players did receive a considerable increase for the occasion.

The semi-final was against Manchester United, also at Hampden Park on the following Saturday, and Celtic fielded an unchanged side. However, the Englishmen, with Matt Busby as their manager, looked formidable. Busby fielded Crompton, McNulty, Aston, Carey, Chilton, Gibson, Viollet, Downie, Rowley, Pearson and Byrne. Johnny Carey was one of the most respected men in football. He had captained the Rest of Europe team against Great Britain on the same ground in 1947, and perhaps diplomatic skills honed in representing both Northern Ireland and Eire had helped him in that multinational and multilingual capacity. By 1953 he was a veteran, as he admitted when he spoke delightfully to a Celtic supporters' rally in Glasgow a year later. 'I decided to retire after the Coronation Cup because I recognised I was slowing down,' he said. 'The first indication was when I was racing back in defence and was passed by the referee. Even worse, later in the game I couldn't keep up with Charlie Tully. It was time to quit then.' Joking aside, Charlie Tully was the man who made both Celtic goals in the 2–1 win over the famed English side, who had eliminated Rangers in the previous round. Perhaps Matt Busby had time to reflect on his club's apparent decision to turn down Tully as a teenager back in 1943.

Celtic had pounded United's goal for the opening 20 minutes before the breakthrough. Tully skipped past McNulty and made as if to cross into the penalty area but instead clipped the ball back to Bertie Peacock. His fellow Ulsterman met the ball in full stride, and his thunderous shot found the net high up.

Only a few minutes into the second half and now facing a strengthening wind, Celtic prepared for a long 45 minutes. Tully again changed things when, just inside his own half in the centre circle, he trapped and controlled a long, awkwardly bouncing clearance from Alec Rollo, and with one deft flick he sent Neil Mochan racing in on the United goal from midfield.

Tully made another noticeable contribution to the semi-final in the very last minute: Manchester United had staged a late rally and Celtic were struggling against the onslaught as well as coping with a strong wind that swept rain into their faces. Tully gathered the ball and wandered towards the corner flag – and this was not a tactic in universal use in the 1950s – where he intended to waste some of the remaining seconds. However, he was dispossessed and slumped to the ground, clutching his leg. Most of the crowd (73,000) assumed that he was not badly injured, if at all, and that he was hoping to play out time while receiving attention on the pitch. The spectators were wrong; he had pulled a muscle and would be unable to play in the Final the following Wednesday. Celtic, of course, won that Coronation Cup Final against Hibernian without the injured Charlie Tully, and with Willie Fernie taking his place.

Tully might well have appreciated the irony of two Scottish clubs – both with Irish roots and founded by Catholic clerics and both wearing the green-and-white – contesting the Final of a competition created to celebrate the accession of a British monarch to the throne. Clearly, he had played a considerable part in getting his club to that Final.

# Notes

1. The Division A clubs competed for the St Mungo Cup, named after the patron saint of Glasgow, while the Division B sides participated in the Quaich – eventually won by Dumbarton.
2. In defence of their 'qualifications', Celtic could have cited Prince Philip, the Duke of Edinburgh, as a precedent. He had married Princess Elizabeth only a year after being granted status as a British subject, and on 16 January 1953 the former naval lieutenant was appointed (on the same day) an admiral of the fleet, a field marshall of the army and a marshall of the Royal Air Force.
3. Celtic's crowds, rounded off, were as follows: 59,000 (Arsenal), 73,000 (Manchester United) and 117,000 (Hibernian) – or about 57 per cent of the aggregate attendance for the entire tournament.

# Chapter 12

## *Breakthrough!*

The 1953–54 season, in which Celtic attained the double of League Championship and Scottish Cup, has to be considered the most meritorious of Charlie Tully's time at Celtic Park. Typically, Celtic followed up the success in the Coronation Cup by failing to qualify from their League Cup section, which included Aberdeen, Airdrie and East Fife, finishing in last place with only two points. Tully could not be held too responsible, as he played in only one fixture (a 1–0 defeat to Aberdeen at Celtic Park on the opening day) and did not appear to have recovered fully from his semi-final injury against Manchester United in the Coronation Cup. He also missed the two first fixtures of the League schedule (a shock 2–0 defeat by Hamilton Academical at Douglas Park and a shaky 1–0 win over Clyde at Celtic Park).

However, he returned for the Old Firm clash at Ibrox on 19 September 1953 at inside-left and contributed to a 1–1 draw. During this match, crowd trouble broke out at the Rangers end of the ground, started when a policeman attempted to remove a Union Jack from a loyalist. At the height of the disturbances, which were fortunately limited to half-time, mounted policemen with batons drawn galloped across the pitch.

Tully, considered match-fit again, appeared in the next home fixture (a 3–0 win over Aberdeen, memorable for Bobby Collins converting three penalty-kicks) and turned out for Northern Ireland against Scotland at Windsor Park on 3 October. In this international, his immediate opponent was Bobby Evans, who had the better of things in Scotland's 3–1 victory.

Throughout October, Charlie Tully made only one appearance for Celtic (in a 1–1 draw against Dundee at Dens Park); he may have been troubled by his muscle strain at times, but it is more likely that Celtic's chronic tinkering with team selection was at fault.

Celtic played 42 matches in the major competitions throughout 1953–54 and had great trouble in settling on the best combination of forwards. In those days the standard formation was as follows: two full-backs, three half-backs and five forwards. Throughout the campaign, Celtic used four players at outside-right and three at inside-right. On the left wing, they used five players at inside-left and five at outside-left; centre-forward apparently still remained the most critical area during this season, however.

Until the arrival of Neil Mochan from Middlesbrough on the eve of the Coronation Cup, Celtic lacked a proven and regular goalscorer. Mochan, initially fielded at centre-forward, was an obvious solution but was selected mainly as a left-winger during his first full season. In all, seven players were chosen to play at centre-forward: John McPhail (15 appearances), Sean Fallon (10), Jimmy Walsh (7), Neil Mochan (4), Sam Hemple (4), Jimmy Duncan (1) and Frank White (1).

One difficulty lay in the fact that Celtic had a number of excellent forwards who could play equally well in a number of positions. Bobby Collins, for example, played in three positions that season and Jimmy Walsh in four. They would have been starters at any other club in the country but, victims of their own versatility, they were excluded from the Scottish Cup side at the end of the season.

A critical game was the fixture against Hibernian at Celtic Park on 7 November, played in pouring rain before a soaked 41,000 crowd. Celtic started well and led through Collins's goal at 20 minutes, but Charlie Tully required prolonged treatment after a heavy tackle; eventually (at 35 minutes), he was carried off on a stretcher.

The match continued with Celtic still enjoying a decent proportion of attacks. But Lawrie Reilly, Hibernian's live wire centre, scored twice within a minute, midway through the second half. Celtic rallied and pounded the visitors' goal to be rewarded with a headed goal from Jock Stein – his first for the club. A draw was an excellent result but still left Celtic tied for third place in the League table with Hearts and Raith Rovers.

Tully would be out of action until 6 February 1954 – an absence of almost 12 weeks. By then, Celtic were still in contention for the League title, five points behind Hearts but with three games in hand. On that date, Celtic travelled to Tynecastle to face the Edinburgh men in what was viewed as a title-decider.

In a typically romantic decision by the chairman, George Hunter was recalled to Celtic's goal, replacing John Bonnar. Hunter, the hero of Celtic's 1951 Scottish Cup campaign with an astonishing display at Tynecastle that eked out a 2–1 win, had been ill and went to Switzerland for recuperation. When he returned, he was never again the goalkeeper he had promised to be, but Bob Kelly felt that an appearance at Tynecastle might kick-start his career.

At half-time the game remained goalless, and Celtic could feel satisfied with a solid defensive display against Hearts' so-called 'Terrible Trio' of Alfie Conn, Willie Bauld and Jimmy Wardhaugh, but the second half exploded into action and drama. Inside the first 15 minutes, Hearts led by 2–0. Both goals were identical, featuring a quick breakaway down the right wing, a high floating cross and a well-directed header from Willie Bauld. Celtic, who had been getting on top, were stunned momentarily but rallied. With only eight minutes left, they had drawn level, as Mike Haughney converted full-blooded drives from the penalty spot.

A draw appeared a fair result for such a hard-fought struggle, but a controversial goal settled the match in Hearts' favour two minutes from the end. Another breakaway down the right wing ended in a high cross into Celtic's goalmouth. Hunter rose confidently enough for it and appeared to have gathered it cleanly at full stretch. Jimmy Wardhaugh challenged for the ball and, with both players high off the ground, shoulder-charged Hunter to bundle him over the goalline – and the referee awarded the 'goal'. Even allowing for the more tolerant approach to physical challenges, the goal simply was not a legitimate one, but it was permitted to stand. Celtic (although still with games in hand) were now seven points behind Hearts with nine matches to play.

Apparently, Bob Kelly endeavoured to cheer up the players on the trip back to Glasgow by asserting that Celtic could still finish ahead of Hearts by the season's end. At the time it did not appear possible. Charlie Tully, absent for much of the season through injury, had reappeared in the Hearts match, and he would play a pivotal role in the season's finale.[1]

The Scottish Cup intervened, and Celtic faced an interesting challenge – a visit to Brockville and a rematch of the previous campaign's heroics. On a heavily sanded pitch on 17 February (after the tie had been postponed from the Saturday), Celtic played cautiously to eke out a 2–1 win, with Fernie and Higgins scoring the goals. Every time Tully went to take a corner-kick, the apprehension in the Falkirk defence was palpable.

Three days later at Celtic Park, the home team gave one of its better performances of the season to rout Dundee by 5–1. Fernie was once again the star, and after he scored Celtic's fourth goal a minute before half-time, Dundee's Billy Steel made a point of congratulating him. Tully was the only forward not to score, but he contributed vastly to the entertainment and the win with his astute distribution. The supporters, leaving the ground at full-time, experienced mixed emotions upon seeing the newspaper headline 'Lucky Rangers', in recognition of the 3–3 draw at Tynecastle. Regardless, it was a vital point dropped by Hearts.

Once again the Scottish Cup intervened, and Celtic were sent to Stirling Albion's Annfield Park, a ground rightly considered a 'bogey'. To the growling displeasure of the vast travelling support, Celtic were two goals down after 25 minutes. Stung by this, they responded with frantic attacks. Haughney scored with a patented blast from the penalty spot, Higgins equalised from close-range after 31 minutes and Neil Mochan put Celtic in front with a thunderbolt from a free-kick. The shot, from fully 35 yards out, was reminiscent of his goal in the Coronation Cup Final. Those three goals, netted within a seven-minute spell, settled the tie in Celtic's favour – and Mochan added a fourth, five minutes into the second half.

Back to League play a week later – on 6 March – Celtic continued to score goals at will in a 4–1 win over East Fife at Parkhead. Once more Tully was selected at inside-left, and once more he provided the openings for the other forwards. Jubilation broke out on the terracing with the news that Hearts had stumbled with a 4–2 defeat at Kirkcaldy.

On 13 March another tense Cup tie beckoned at Douglas Park (where Celtic had lost on the first day of the season), and Hamilton Academical, by now doomed to relegation, put up a grim fight to stay in the Scottish Cup. Celtic eventually won by 2–1, but it was a highly unpleasant affair, and the *Evening Times* reported that Willie Fernie alone had been fouled 15 times. Among the culprits was Accies' young full-back Bobby Shearer (who would, of course, resume hostilities later with Neil Mochan in Old Firm matches).

Tully had also been the victim of heavy tackling in the Cup tie at Hamilton and was rested for the League game at Broomfield on St Patrick's Day, with Bobby Collins taking his place. Other changes were made: Mike Haughney had been chosen for a League international, and he was replaced by Alec Boden, making his first appearance of the season; Jock Stein had been in the wars at Douglas Park and was unfit, Jim McIlroy substituting for him; Jimmy Walsh was also missing, and his spot at centre-forward was taken by Sean Fallon, always a favourite of the chairman thanks to his wholehearted play. It was another of Bob Kelly's 'hunches', and this one worked: Celtic won comfortably by 6–0 against Airdrie. Mochan, by now a fixture at outside-left, scored three times, and Fallon netted the third goal on the stroke of half-time.

On 20 March the tide turned in Celtic's favour, although for a long time the odds were against it. Celtic went to Firhill to face a Partick Thistle side who still entertained some hopes of winning the title, and Tully was still not available. It proved to be an old-fashioned thriller with Thistle scoring in only three minutes and dominating throughout an exciting first half, played on a heavy, muddy pitch. John Bonnar had to reproduce his form of the Coronation Cup Final to keep Thistle at bay, a string of saves denying the Jags time and time again.

At half-time, the mood in the Celtic dressing room was funereal. They were a goal down, without their brainiest inside-forward, and with Jimmy Walsh limping on the left wing. To add to that, Neil Mochan was injured and had to move to the other wing. With no substitutes allowed, it was expected of injured players to soldier on.

What changed this match? The first thing was the constant roar of encouragement from the supporters, which was increased with the news, just after half-time, that Hearts were also trailing at Pittodrie…and Celtic were responding, no player more so than Sean Fallon, who was gradually getting the better of a physical duel with Jimmy Davidson. He equalised at 64 minutes amid tremendous excitement, and Willie Fernie finished off one of his characteristic runs along the byline by blasting the ball past Ledgerwood. A wonderful comeback was completed when Fallon galloped through the tiring Thistle defence, shrugging off tackles like Jimmy Quinn at the turn of the century, to score a third goal. And Hearts lost at Pittodrie!

A stutter in the Scottish Cup followed, with Celtic drawing 2–2 against Motherwell in the semi-final before a crowd of 102,000. Sean Fallon continued with his unlikely goalscoring heroics, but a last-minute equaliser earned Motherwell a replay. That was on the Saturday (27 March), and a League fixture against Stirling Albion followed on the Monday evening. Charlie Tully, still not 100 per cent fit, was rested for this match, and

Celtic were comfortable winners by 4–0. He was missing again for the replay against Motherwell at Hampden Park, having narrowly failed a late fitness test. Celtic, however, ran out comfortable winners by 3–1, despite Mike Haughney spoiling his record from the penalty spot late on. John Higgins was outstanding in this replay, as he had been in the first match, and this meant that Bobby Collins would not be picked at outside-right for the Cup Final.

Tully returned for the match at Love Street against St Mirren and celebrated with the first goal in a 3–1 win. It was a quiet game, as Celtic scored two goals within four minutes early in the first half, settling the outcome, but the victory meant that Celtic went to the top of the League for the first time that season, and they would stay there while Hearts continued to struggle. At the end of the season Celtic won the League title by a healthy margin of five points.

The Scottish Cup Final was played on 24 April 1954 before a crowd of 129,926, and Aberdeen were the opponents. Celtic ran out narrow winners by 2–1. The deciding goal was scored by Sean Fallon at 63 minutes after a typically mazy run by Fernie, who had meandered down the right wing and along the byline before squaring the ball to the Irishman. It was Celtic's first double since 1914, and it was celebrated in style.

What had gone right? In the first place, Celtic had a reasonably solid defence, performing unchanged for much of the season. Bonnar regained a measure of consistency, although he had been challenged earlier on by Bell and Hunter; Haughney and Meechan were two old-fashioned full-backs who tackled hard and cleared their lines as their first priority; Jock Stein was the organiser in defence and, as captain, was effective in eventually making Celtic a difficult team to beat; and on his either side, Celtic had two world-class wing-halves in Bobby Evans and Bertie Peacock. Evans, since his conversion to the half-back line, had always performed with distinction, but Peacock, first played at left-half in a 1–1 draw at Ibrox on 19 September, had flourished. As indicated earlier in the chapter, Celtic did have problems in selecting the right combination of forwards, but they had reached a recognised line up by the end of the season.

For the first time in Charlie Tully's career at Celtic Park, he had the luxury of playing in a settled team and a reasonably successful one. It was only at the tail end of the season and at the start of the Scottish Cup campaign that Tully, out injured for so long, was restored to the side, and the results speak for themselves. During that late run of 15 matches without defeat, Celtic fielded their three Irishmen – Tully, Peacock and Fallon – to great effect. Charlie Tully played exclusively at inside-left, a position from which he was expected to hold the ball, to create openings and to dictate the pace of the game. As a midfield general (to use the modern phrase), he was exceptional and played a considerable part in the race towards the double.

Bertie Peacock had started the season in his regular position of inside-left and had played, as always, with limited success. He was a hard worker, rather derogatorily referred to as 'the labourer', but he was enthusiastic, willing and incredibly fit, prepared to run, chase and harry all 90 minutes. It seems obvious now that he was a half-back masquerading as an inside-forward, but his selection at left-half caused consternation among the supporters when first announced. Like other Celts before and after him (Evans, Fernie and Murdoch), he was a revelation when moved backwards.

Sean Fallon, regularly employed as either right or left-back, had played for Eire as a stop-gap centre-forward before being selected for Celtic in that role. His introduction had come in the St Mungo Cup, and his rampaging style had caused defenders trouble, but he seemed to be effective only in the short term. However, given an extended run as a forward in 1953–54, he made 10 successive appearances and scored seven goals.

As this book deals with the life and times of one Charles Patrick Tully, generally recognised as an archetypal Irishman, it might be worth looking briefly at Bertie Peacock and Sean Fallon in this context. Bertie Peacock was a credit to the game in every possible way. Unlike Tully, he did not make an immediate impact; he was a player of some promise, but he had to work hard to break into Celtic's side and to hold his place. He was a serious, hard-grafting player who impressed with his effort and commitment. Once he had adjusted to the pace of the Scottish game, he was able to show his skill – but he was never a Tully nor a Fernie in that department. Like Tully, he was an Ulsterman, but from the other side of the religious and social divide in the province. Thanks to his character (and effort), that never became an issue with any supporters. Throughout a long and distinguished career with Celtic (from 1949 to 1961), he made 453 appearances in the major competitions.

Sean Fallon, a sturdy, no-nonsense full-back, was a different type of Irishman from Tully in that he presented himself as an earnest young man throughout his Celtic career. Never considered an outstanding player, Fallon was still an internationalist and represented his chosen country (Eire) well in his eight appearances. Like Peacock – and unlike Tully – he never allowed himself to be a controversial figure on the field, and perhaps he could be best described as a journeyman. The future would unveil other differences.

Charlie Tully, the most naturally talented of the three Irishmen and the most charismatic, shone on the field of play, and off it. After leaving Glasgow, Charlie returned to the Falls Road in Belfast, feted as a local hero and recognised as 'a character'. His public life largley over, his stints as a manager were mere footnotes to his career.

Bertie Peacock and Sean Fallon remained within football and contributed to the sport for a long time after they retired as performers. Sean's greatest contribution to

Celtic would lie off the field as a coach under Jimmy McGrory and as assistant manager to Jock Stein. Bertie, after his return to Northern Ireland, attained the chairmanship of Coleraine and high office within the Greater Coleraine Council. They — Sean and Bertie — would earn lasting respect through their sterling character and work ethic, whereas Charlie Tully earned love and affection simply because he was Charlie Tully.

Perhaps inevitably in the nature of things, Charlie died young (at 47), Bertie died suddenly in his late seventies, although apparently in excellent health, and Sean Fallon is still alive and well at the age of 86.

## Note

1. During the run-in for the double, Tully played in six of the nine League games, and Celtic won all six. He missed only one of Celtic's six Scottish Cup ties. Of these 12 matches, in which he played at the most critical stage of the season, Celtic remained undefeated, winning 11 and drawing one.

## Chapter 13

# —— *The Last Hurrah – and the Greatest* ——

So often in the 1950s, Celtic succeeded in hamstringing themselves on vital occasions by picking the wrong team – or permutation. The problem, of course, lay in the relationship between a dictatorial chairman and a diffident manager. In the words of the terracing 'know-it-alls', Jimmy McGrory was little more than 'Bob Kelly's office boy'. Simply put, Bob Kelly picked the team and Jimmy McGrory invariably bowed to his wishes. The trouble was that Kelly had never played the game at any level other than a few games with Blantyre Victoria, but this experience and faithful attendance at Celtic matches for decades, along with an inflated sense of his own expertise, allowed the chairman to continue his practice without much self-examination. The inevitable setbacks (such as defeats in successive Scottish Cup Finals), he simply shrugged off. In the feudal structure of football clubs, players and managers had to accept such practices.

Celtic were a side for the short run, not the long haul, and this was never better illustrated than between 1956 and 1957 in the League Cup. Celtic won the League Cup for the first time in 1956–57, and Charlie Tully played an important part. Against Rangers in the sectional play, and a few minutes after Haughney had missed a penalty, Tully scored the winning goal in a 2–1 win. It was a masterpiece of quick thinking. Following a partially cleared corner from the right, Tully gathered the ball with his back to Rangers' goal. Instead of trapping the ball, he allowed it to bounce and then lobbed it over his head towards the goal. The gambit, virtually impossible to defend, saw the ball dip into the net at the far junction of the post and crossbar.

Celtic met Partick Thistle in the Final, and the result was a disappointing 0–0 draw, with Celtic's forwards weaving too many patterns without a definite conclusion. Tully again produced his best form for the replay on 31 October 1956. The *Glasgow Herald* (1 November 1956) described his performance: 'Sooner or later, one felt, this mercurial player who was having one of his best days of dexterous ball-control, astute passing, intelligent crossing and corner-kicking would contrive such a scoring chance as not even his finicky colleagues could squander.' In the end, Celtic won comfortably, 3–0, with all the goals coming in the second half.

In the sectional play in 1957–58, Airdrie offered stuffy opposition in Celtic's bid to retain the trophy. It was the sort of resistance that often proved fatal to Celtic's progress, but Charlie Tully, although considered a veteran, was instrumental in bailing them out. The match on the opening day of the season (10 August 1957) ended in a narrow 3–2 win, and the mood on the terracing was far from happy. The game was played amid torrential rain, which forced thousands among the 38,000 attendance to seek shelter under the new cantilevered cover at the Celtic end of ground. The dreaded slow handclap resounded as Celtic struggled, before they equalised at 2–2 at 70 minutes. Tully meandered along the byline and cut the ball back to Collins, who slipped the ball to Mochan, who fired home. The reporter for the *Daily Record*, former Celtic centre-forward John McPhail, commented acidly 'If that's Tully finished, the others have qualified for a pension!'

Tully's contribution to the Broomfield match was even more decisive. According to the *Sunday Express* on 25 August 1957, 'nobody else used the cross-field pass so well. Nobody else kept his opponents turning so often on this slippery turf.' A goal down after 20 minutes in another downpour, Celtic fought back. Eric Smith headed the equaliser from Tully's corner at 44 minutes, while another Tully corner at 72 minutes was glided on by McPhail's head and finished with a volley from Willie Fernie.

Approaching the League Cup Final against Rangers on 19 October 1957, Celtic were faced with some problems in selection. Who would be chosen by Bob Kelly? Billy McPhail, the hero of the previous season's triumph in the competition, was experiencing some twinges in his knee – the chronic condition that had hampered him throughout his career. For the League match against Raith Rovers a week before the Cup Final, he had been rested and replaced by Neil Mochan. Fringe players, such as the talented Jim Sharkey and the promising Jim Conway, may have flitted across the chairman's mind, but in the end he opted for experience. Billy McPhail would lead the line.

On the left wing, combative youngster Bertie Auld, after missing the first three League Cup ties, had been chosen for the next six games, including the semi-final won 4–2 over Clyde at Ibrox on 28 September. He was the man in possession, but he had not endeared himself to Bob Kelly with his 'gallus' outlook. He would be in direct opposition to Rangers' Bobby Shearer, a full-back scarcely famed for taking prisoners, and flare-ups could be expected in that area. In a recent Old Firm clash at Ibrox, Shearer had shown himself to be no respecter of reputations in a typically robust display against Charlie Tully, who had not relished the physical confrontations with the sturdy defender. Auld was too young and prone to retaliation; Tully was experienced but considered a shade fragile. In the end, the chairman decided to recall Neil Mochan to the left-wing position. Ironically, Mochan had never been a personal favourite of Kelly's and had frequently been dropped, although he was the club's most consistent goalscorer.

Another problem emerged in the days before the Final, and that was a difference of opinion between Bobby Evans and Charlie Tully – two of the most experienced men in the side. A difference of opinion is an understatement, because both men came to blows in the dressing room at Celtic Park before a training session. The immediate cause was the Irishman's

'TULLYvision' column in the *Evening Citizen*, and the irony lay in the fact that Tully did not actually write it himself, as a journalist 'ghosted' the articles after conversations with him. However, they did contain his views to a certain extent.

Two weeks earlier, Northern Ireland and Scotland had drawn a tedious match at Windsor Park, and Tully felt bound to comment on it: 'Scotland, instead of going forward, aren't even standing still. They're going backwards…Whether you people over here like it or not, only two Scots would have a chance of a place in any Great Britain eleven. These two are (Tommy) Younger (Hibernian) and (Alec) Parker (Falkirk). The rest lack class…I fancy I'll get my head in my hands for interfering but I had to have my say' (*Evening Citizen*, 12 October 1957).

By 1957 Tully was no longer a regular for Northern Ireland, but Bobby Evans was still chosen consistently for Scotland. The two men were like chalk and cheese: Evans a Roundhead and Tully a Cavalier. Evans was serious, determined and touchy, and Tully light-hearted, casual and teasing. At their best on the football pitch, Bobby Evans was the heart of Celtic, while Tully was its intelligence. According to Tully's own account, Evans resented the article and felt it belittled him in print. Apparently, he cut it out of the paper and pinned it to the wall in the dressing room, adding a few choice comments of his own. Eventually, the matter reached a confrontation – and astonishingly (only a few days before an Old Firm Cup Final), the pair came to blows. They were separated by teammates after what Tully described as 'a scene from a John Wayne film'. Had the chairman heard about the fight, he might well have dropped both players from the Cup Final team – and Rangers would have been overwhelming favourites for that Final – but the matter was hushed up among the players, and the chairman left in blissful ignorance.

To give Bob Kelly his due, he did select the right Celtic team for this particular occasion, with Billy McPhail restored to centre-forward, Neil Mochan preferred to Bertie Auld on the left wing and Charlie Tully on the right.

**Celtic:** Beattie, Donnelly, Fallon, Fernie, Evans, Peacock, Tully, Collins, McPhail, Wilson, Mochan.

**Rangers:** Niven, Shearer, Caldow, McColl, Valentine, Davis, Scott, Simpson, Murray, Baird, Hubbard.

Although the weather had improved considerably in the hours before the kick-off, the pitch remained a shade heavy — conditions that seemed to favour the more physically inclined Rangers. Bertie Peacock won the toss and chose to shoot into the King's Park end of Hampden, where the majority of Celtic supporters were congregated.

A few minutes after the kick-off, Cyril Horne, the principal football writer for the *Glasgow Herald*, stroked his chin thoughtfully and turned to the man beside him in the press box. 'You know, at this moment it looks as if Caldow is going to play Tully cleanly. This could be very interesting...' To be perfectly honest, that was no great surprise, as Eric Caldow was a scrupulously honest full-back and a fine sportsman.

Those spectators in the Celtic end could scarcely complain of being deprived of the action, as Celtic totally dominated that first half. A two-goal lead at the interval was a shabby reward for such dominance: within the opening 20 minutes, Bobby Collins had struck the post with Niven hopelessly beaten, and Tully had come within inches of what one newspaper described as 'the goal of the century', when he drifted effortlessly past several floundering defenders and released a shot-cum-cross-cum-lob that bewildered Niven, but which struck the inside of one post before rebounding across the face of the empty goal and going behind the other post for a goal-kick.

In *Oh, Hampden in the Sun* — a book devoted exclusively to this one match — the authors (Peter Burns and Pat Woods) quote a fan, Charlie Harvey:

*Tully was denied what would undoubtedly have been the best goal of all time. At the angle of the penalty box, over on the stand side, he stood with his right foot on the ball as two worried 'Gers defenders sprinted towards him. They went in different directions as Charlie waggled his arse while moving the ball forward, back and then sideways. It was done on about one yard square of turf. Never famous for his shot, he took a couple of steps forward and hit a rocket that beat Niven at his near post. The ball struck the inside of the upright, travelled the length of the goalline, hit the other post, and came out. At that moment, many a devout man uttered very bad sweary words.*

It was one indication that Charlie Tully was going to have one of his great days, as 'Waverley' indicated on the Monday: 'The Irishman may be a bit of a kidder but here he was in deadly earnest, almost serious-minded and purposeful, never the jester. Shedding his happy-go-lucky image, he tormented his opponents with an exhibition of thoughtful manoeuvring and passing, as if to give a two-fingered salute to critics who had dismissed him as entertaining but ineffective' (*Daily Record*, 21 October 1957).

After 23 minutes of such pressure, Celtic finally scored. Billy McPhail was proving the master of Valentine in the air, and he headed the ball back and down to his new-found partner, Sammy Wilson, who volleyed it home from 12 yards out. By this stage, Rangers had been reduced to desperate defending to stop a rampant Celtic whose wing-halves, Fernie and Peacock (displaying the skills of the inside-forwards they once had been), were joining in every attack. Only three minutes after the opening goal, Bobby Collins smashed a free-kick from 30 yards out against the crossbar with George Niven beaten again. The fear was that a one-goal lead at half-time would constitute a meagre reward, that the Ibrox men would have time to regroup at the interval and would have the wind behind them in the second half, and Celtic — worthy of a four-goal lead — would regret not punishing their opponents more severely.

Neil Mochan did much to settle those doubts in the last minute of the half after Billy McPhail — a wielder of a rapier rather than a claymore — gathered a pass from Wilson and languidly released another pass down the left wing, where Mochan gathered it and raced past McColl and Shearer. He blasted the ball past Niven with a rising shot from the narrowest of angles. Mochan had also troubled Rangers in that first half with his running and readiness to shoot, but he did more psychological damage when he showed his physical edge over the Ibrox right-back Bobby Shearer — known as 'Captain Cutlass' for his uncompromisingly robust approach. On that occasion Shearer attempted to charge Mochan over the touchline, but the sturdy Celtic winger stood his ground and it was Shearer who was sent crashing to the ground. The referee Mr J.A. Mowat, who had been a regular at Old Firm clashes for a number of years, was strict but he was old-fashioned enough to recognise that shoulder-charging was a legitimate practice under the rules and did not give the highly embarrassed Shearer the consolation of a free-kick.

With hindsight — when vision is always 20–20 — that two-goal lead should have been enough for Celtic to retain the League Cup. It was the Parkhead men who were winning the individual clashes all over that Hampden pitch. Charlie Tully, slower than in his heyday but infinitely more cunning, was at his most deceptive. Time after time he would gather the ball, and Rangers defenders could not fathom if he would dribble or pass. He did both to devastating effect and, not for the first time, this supreme individualist resorted to becoming a team player. Neil Mochan had imposed himself on Bobby Shearer with both strength and skill, and McColl was increasingly being drawn out of position to help his full-back. Billy McPhail had won every ball in the air and had the beating of John Valentine whenever he held the ball, even on the ground.

By the end of the match, Valentine – who had been a stalwart so often for Queen's Park on this pitch and who had been seen as the natural replacement for the retired George Young and the suspended Willie Woodburn – was totally flustered. In fact, he was never chosen for Rangers again.

Bobby Collins had been desperately unlucky with two shots that struck woodwork, but he had had an influence on the measure of Celtic's superiority. A tireless worker and a hard little man, Collins had sprayed passes all over the Hampden pitch, and the reliable Harold Davis, himself a physical player, had no means of stopping him. Even in defence, Celtic were winning those vital duels. Bobby Evans at centre-half was immaculate and scarcely gave Murray a kick of the ball. Evans's anticipation allowed him to stop the isolated Rangers foray with such ease it was made to look more inept than it was.

Sean Fallon, Celtic's 'Iron Man', had established a psychological mastery over Rangers' skilful right-winger Alec Scott earlier in the Ibrox man's career, and he once more imposed himself on the youngster without having to be overly physical. Bertie Peacock was another immense figure for Celtic, busy as ever and joining in attacks, but that was only after he had mastered his Northern Ireland colleague Billy Simpson.

But one player above all was coming on to the game of his life – Willie Fernie. The quiet man from Fife, originally an inside-right and a skilful dribbler, had played several forward positions for Celtic – and indeed Scotland – but he found himself as a wing-half. This seems to be a Parkhead tradition, as Bobby Evans before him and Bobby Murdoch after him also developed into world-class performers when they moved back into the right-half position. To the delight of the Celtic following, Fernie ignored Sammy Baird as an attacking threat and forced the Ranger, never the most popular of figures among Celtic supporters, to defend instead, but Willie Fernie was unstoppable that October day. Baird had to resort to crude tackling in efforts to stop him, but Fernie continued to beat both Baird and Davis time after time, leaving the Ibrox men trailing hopelessly in his wake and disconcerting Caldow, who also had Charlie Tully to deal with. Tully, himself on top form, was the ideal foil for Fernie's rampaging runs down the right. The Irishman simply could not be ignored by Rangers' overworked defenders, and this left more room for Fernie's advances.

The second half was sheer bliss for Celtic and their support, from the moment (at 53 minutes) when Billy McPhail rose to a perfect cross from Collins and headed the ball almost casually past Niven. However, Rangers did raise hopes among their following when Simpson scored with a diving header five minutes later. It was a splendid goal, but the hard hearts among Celtic's supporters pointed out that the goal was scored while Bobby Evans was off the pitch to receive medical attention.

Ten minutes after Simpson's goal, the match was over as a contest. Celtic had continued to swarm into attack, and Rangers became increasingly disorientated in defence. One gloating Celtic fan said the Ibrox defenders were 'as organised as a tossed salad', and that description seemed apt in the wake of Celtic's fourth goal. Billy McPhail had just rammed the ball into the roof of the net after gathering a loose ball six yards out, and the photograph showed the disarray among Rangers defenders: Niven, admittedly a gallant 'keeper throughout, sprawled helplessly on his back; Shearer flat on his stomach and with his face buried in the Hampden turf; Valentine, in the foreground, helpless to intervene and turning away; and McColl, in the background, with an agonised expression on his face and body language indicating that a heavy defeat was now almost certain.

The agony continued for Rangers as Celtic, totally dominant now, continued to press forward with every man eager for the ball. What was most pleasing for the Celtic support among the 82,293 crowd – apart from the score and the sight of their Ibrox counterparts leaving in droves – was the undeniable fact that Celtic had been administering a football masterclass from the opening whistle and yet seemed to be moving into a higher gear.

Another neat move down the right wing resulted in Sammy Wilson receiving the ball in his inside-left position, and he quickly swept it over to Mochan, who lashed the ball into the far corner of the net. It was scarcely a perfect strike from the hardest shot in Scottish football, as he did not make great contact with the ball but rather drove it into the ground, yet it was strong enough to elude Niven. The Celtic end of Hampden was past caring about perfection, however, as they erupted once more behind Beattie's goal. That was at 75 minutes, and 15 minutes remained for Rangers to endure – at least for the players on the pitch, who could hardly depart the scene with the same haste as their followers.

Five minutes passed before the next goal, which was an individual effort from Billy McPhail. Beattie was called into action to receive a pass-back and punted the ball downfield where, once again, McPhail beat Valentine in the air. Both players stumbled upon landing, but McPhail was first to recover and raced away from the centre circle, veering slightly to the right as he advanced upon a surely shell-shocked George Niven. In that almost casual style of his, McPhail took his time, considered the options and beat Niven with a rising shot at the 'keeper's left-hand post. That was the last straw for some among the thinning crowd at the Mount Florida end. In their rage, bottles were thrown, fighting broke out, hundreds escaped to the relative safety of the running track, and police (200 of them, according to reports) rushed to avert worse trouble. In the turmoil, 17 were arrested (and 11 injured), and to some at the other end of the ground the spectacle added to the enjoyment. A lollipop lady could have controlled the thousands of Celtic supporters massed behind the far goal as they relished every passing moment and were by now singing every song in the repertoire – and perhaps already thinking of composing new ones to mark the occasion.

Confusion was reigning in the Ibrox penalty area, and Shearer pulled down Billy McPhail from behind in the last minute. After inviting McPhail to take the kick, Willie

Fernie — the coolest and most accomplished performer on the pitch — stepped up. In his own words, 'I wasn't too sure where I would place the ball, but I noticed the 'keeper's bunnet in the corner of the net — and aimed for that.' Seconds later he hit it, Hampden erupted into green-and-white for the seventh time that afternoon and Celtic's goalkeeper Dick Beattie raised seven fingers in the air as Jack Mowat blew the final whistle.

A few days later Mr Mowat bumped into Rangers' PR officer, former journalist Willie Allison, in a Glasgow street. Allison said 'Jack, it was bad enough on Saturday, but did you need to give them a penalty as well just to rub it in?' Mowat's reply was 'But, Mr Allison, it *was* a penalty.'

Charlie Tully could leave the Hampden pitch and receive his medal with quiet satisfaction. He had played a major part in the rout but in a different manner from the flamboyance of past seasons. He had roasted young Caldow and spread panic among a Rangers rearguard, who dreaded what he might do next. None of them wanted to be embarrassed publicly by one of the most skilled dribblers in the game, balding and slow as he now was. They were glad to leave him alone, and Tully revelled in the space. With time to control the ball, he held it until either Collins or Fernie moved into position and then released it with subtle but devastating results. Astonishingly, for such a polished performance by the veteran, his actual participation in the seven goals scored was minimal; despite that oddity, he has to be rated as one of the best performers on the park. An Irishism, surely.

It was a night for celebration — a result that many Celtic adherents rate even higher than the 1967 triumph in Lisbon. The Celtic party headed for its favourite Glasgow restaurant and Bob Kelly, quietly jubilant at his rare tactical permutation, was considerate enough to remember an absent player. Jock Stein, who had listened to the match on the radio at his Hamilton home, was recuperating from yet another operation on his damaged ankle. Kelly arranged for a car to be sent to Hamilton to pick up the former captain. It might not be too much to suggest that such gestures within the Celtic family did much to make Jock Stein realise that he had found a home for life at Celtic Park.

The Celtic family were all there that night at the festivities in Ferrari's. Charlie Tully found himself beside Bobby Evans, with whom he had squabbled a few days previously and with whom he had never been personally close. But both men had given sterling service to Celtic and had performed immaculately at Hampden that afternoon, combining to inflict a humiliating defeat upon the club's greatest rivals. Tully also mingled with Jock Stein who, as Celtic's captain, had little patience with some aspects of Charlie's attitude as a player. Stein also admitted later that as Celtic's manager 'I would have had to chase Charlie away as a player in my Celtic teams – a pity though.' Also at the table that night were fellow Irishmen Bertie Peacock and Sean Fallon, a Sligo man, who described himself thus: 'I was just an ordinary player with only a big heart and a fighting spirit to recommend me.' And it might be worthwhile pointing out in passing that it was a team that included players, in almost equal numbers, from both sides of the religious divide that has scarred both Scotland and Ireland in the past. For instance, the half-back line of Evans, Stein and Peacock – all Celtic captains at one time – were Protestants, but many Celtic supporters would consider that trio as one of the best in the club's history. But the times were a-changing.

While many Celtic supporters of a certain vintage can recite flawlessly the Celtic line up at Hampden that 19 October 1957, it is interesting to relate that the chosen side played only eight matches as a unit – and won them all. Four of the games were prior to the Final and all were in the League Cup run: East Fife (6–1), Hibernian (2–0), Third Lanark (6–1 and 3–0). Three of the games were after the 7–1 game and in the League campaign: East Fife (3–0), Hibernian (1–0) and Airdrie (5–2). In fact, it was a short-lived run starting with a 6–1 win over East Fife on 28 August and ending with a 5–2 win against Airdrie on 30 November, a few weeks after the Hampden triumph.

The match at Airdrie on 30 November 1957 was a turning point in Charlie Tully's career. He damaged a thigh muscle in his right leg through over-stretching for a wayward pass. He felt that the injury required rest rather than exercise, and this was an opinion borne out by a specialist after the exercises failed to clear up the damage. However, the Celtic backroom staff had insisted on exercise, with the result that Tully – who had played in the first 18 matches of the season – made only one further token appearance (against St Mirren on 8 March 1958) that season.

Obviously, despite the subtlety of his performance against Rangers in that League Cup Final, Charlie Tully's career with Celtic – as with almost all veteran players – was in decline. Now 33 and a player not noted for application in training, he was increasingly prone to injury. Sadly, the great Irishman and Celtic star was to fade quietly into the background – a bit like a matinee idol taking cameo roles to prolong his career while emerging talents sought the spotlight.

# Chapter 14

## —————— *Rangers and Other Opponents* ——————

When Charlie Tully joined Celtic in 1948, football in Scotland was relatively static, as every side favoured a 2–3–5 formation. This comprised two full-backs (who rarely ventured over the halfway line), three half-backs and five forwards, playing in a W formation. Frequently the centre-half played behind his wing-halves and closer to his full-backs, thus he was often termed 'the pivot'.

Changes in personnel from week to week were infrequent and usually due only to injury. Transfers of players between senior clubs were rare, and every year most clubs would announce with some fanfare that a promising junior or two would be moving up to join them. Many football fans, now in their seventies, can still probably recite the line ups in those days with very few mistakes: Brown, Young, Shaw, McColl, Woodburn, Cox (Rangers)…Smith, Johnstone, Reilly, Turnbull, Ormond (Hibernian)…Johnstone, Kilmarnock, Shaw, McLeod, Paton, Redpath (Motherwell) – the names trip off the tongue. However, a Celtic line up might be more difficult, as changes, often at the whim of the chairman, were made frequently.

In the early 1950s it was also possible to line up a football team in their street clothes and estimate their positions strictly by their physical appearance, as one columnist claimed 'the full-backs were short, squat men with prison haircuts, no-nonsense faces and fearsome legs'. Another contemporary critic suggested that these full-backs were 'hewn rather than born', and the equipment that footballers had did not help the more skilled forwards. Tom Finney, one of the greatest of all English wingers, recalled 'Boots? Those boots. Remember? Stiff leather up over the ankles, bulbous toe-caps. Felt like diver's boots. When it rained and the shirt collected the water and the socks were soaked, we must have weighed a ton a piece. Don't know how we moved.'

Sean Fallon, himself a determined full-back with Celtic, told me:

*Neil Mochan and Charlie Tully alternated frequently on the left wing; Mochan was usually preferred against strong physical full-backs – and that was what happened in the 7–1 League Cup Final, with Rangers playing Bobby Shearer at right-back. But Charlie could be cute when he faced such a defender. He would not attempt to hold the ball, but he would pass it and usually it was an intelligent pass. Even when two or three were put on to him, he had such a good football brain he wouldn't try to take them all on, but he would take them out of the game with one shrewd pass that left them stranded. It was no disadvantage when Charlie was being man-marked by a strong, robust full-back – a man such as Don Emery of Aberdeen, a man with legs like tree trunks.*

Mention of Don Emery reminded me to look up other right-backs of the time, and almost all of them were sturdy, no-nonsense types with some verging on the intimidating: Balunas (Third Lanark), Follon (Dundee), Gibson (Clyde), Govan (Hibernian), Howie (Hibernian), Kilmarnock (Motherwell), Lapsley (St Mirren), Parker (Hearts), McClure (Raith Rovers), McGowan (Partick Thistle), Mitchell (Morton), Young (Rangers) and more.

Some of these full-backs were entrusted with the taking of penalty-kicks, perhaps because a lack of imagination would prevent too much dwelling on the consequences of missing. Most (including Mike Haughney of Celtic) favoured a long run-up and a fierce shot. Jock Stein once foiled Dave Lapsley of St Mirren after the visitors had been given a dubious penalty-kick at Celtic Park on 12 December 1953. Lapsley's custom was to have a colleague place the ball for him on the spot and to start his approach from midfield. Stein, well aware of the tactic and still disgruntled about the referee's decision, placed himself casually just outside the penalty area but in a direct line between Lapsley and the ball. The St Mirren full-back, who had switched from a trot into a run, was forced to break stride to go round Stein and hesitated as if to reconsider but half-decided to continue – only to shank the ball far wide of the post. Stein remained unrepentant: 'The rules say I have to give him 10 yards. Where does it say I have to give him 50?'

In his novel *From Scenes Like These*, Gordon Williams's main character appears to be one who recognised that Scottish football had declined, with sides and individual players relying on physique rather than skill:

*That was the greatest thing he could imagine in the whole world, being picked against England – he'd die for Scotland. It was just a pity that the Scottish selectors were blinded by Glasgow Rangers. Great players with small clubs didn't stand a chance of being picked for Scotland if there was some six-foot Tarzan at Ibrox Park. Rangers didn't even play like real Scots yet they dominated the whole game because they had the big money. Hibs played like Scots, tricky, clever, artistic – yet Gordon Smith, the great 'Gay Gordon' who could do anything with a ball, hardly ever got capped for Scotland. Willie McNaught was the classiest left-back in the game, but because he played for Raith Rovers he never got a look in. Jimmy Mason of Third Lanark, small and round-shouldered and insignificant until he got the ball, had helped Scotland beat England three–one at Wembley – but how many caps did he get after that?[1]*

Best Wishes
Charlie Tully

*Giving or receiving? Charlie at a supporters' club function.*

*Posing in his Ireland strip. (1951)*

*Charlie captains Glasgow Celtic, and his friend Jackie Vernon captains 'Belfast Celtic' for a friendly in May 1952.*

*Concentrating in an Old Firm Cup tie at Ibrox.*
*(1953)*

*Neil Mochan turns away after scoring the only goal of the 1954 Ne'erday clash at Celtic Park. (1954)*

*Taking on the full-back at Celtic Park.*

*It takes practice to score from a corner-kick. (1955)*

*Foiled by George Niven in an Old Firm Charity Cup tie. (1955)*

*Stein leads out Celtic for the Scottish Cup Final, followed by Bonnar, Tully, Haughney and Walsh. (1955)*

*Keeping a watchful eye on the goalkeeper.*

THIS **Minute of Agreement** entered into
between           JAMES McGRORY     MANAGER
Secretary of, and as representing
           CELTIC FOOTBALL           Club,
Limited, duly authorised to enter into this Agreement on behalf of the said Club (hereinafter called
"the club"); and     Charles Patrick Tully
residing at         174, Randolph Drive,
           Clarkston.
(hereinafter called "the player"); witnesseth that
the parties have agreed as follows :—

---

9. In consideration of the services and of the observance by the player of the terms and conditions of this Agreement the club shall pay to the player the sum of     Fourteen Pounds          (£ 14 :   : ) per week from     29th April 1955          to the termination hereof.

Fill in any Special Provisions required

Fourteen Pounds (£14) per week in the playing season and Eleven Pounds (£11) per week in the closed season subject to a bonus of One Pound (£1) per point when playing in the First Team, and ten shillings per point when playing in the Second Team.

10. This Agreement shall expire (unless same is sooner terminated under Articles 3rd, 7th or 8th hereof) on the     31st     day of     July     Nineteen hundred and     Fifty-six (56)

---

IN WITNESS WHEREOF: these presents are subscribed in duplicate for and on behalf of the said Football Club, Limited, by the said     James McGrory     Manager     as secretary thereof, and by the said     Charles Patrick Tully     at     Celtic Park     on the     29th     day of     April     Nineteen hundred and     Fifty-five (55)     before these witnesses

Audrey Douglas          (Shorthand Typist)

Fill in Names, Designations and Addresses of Witnesses

28, Second Avenue.Glasgow.S.4.
George Paterson          (Coach)
35, Garve Avenue.Glasgow.S.4.

*Andrey Douglas* witness.          *Charles Patrick Tully*
*George Paterson (Coach)* witness.          STAMP     *James McGrory*

*Excerpts from Charlie's contract. (1956)*

*Decades before Eric Cantona, Charlie Tully preferred his collar turned up. (1956)*

*On tour in the United States. (1956)*

*Style icon?*
*(both from 1957)*

# CELTIC

## Official Programme

NEIL MOCHAN

**SCOTTISH CUP—1st ROUND**

# CELTIC v. ALBION ROVERS

Saturday, 31st January, 1959

Kick-off 3 p.m.

No. 13                                        PRICE THREEPENCE

*Charlie's last game. (1959)*

*Unwinding after a home win.*

*The family group in Glasgow: Charlie and Carrie, Charlie Jr and Patricia.*

*Bobby Evans – international opponent and Celtic teammate.*

*Willie Fernie: along with Charlie, he tore Rangers to shreds in the 1957 League Cup Final.*

*A visit to the old Celtic Park in Belfast for Charlie and Jackie Vernon.*

*Jock Stein as Celtic's manager. Although an admirer, he could never contemplate having Charlie in one of his sides.*

*Retired? Charlie works out with his son in Belfast.*

*On good terms with the clergy.*

# MY LORD AND MY GOD

In loving memory of

## CHARLES P. TULLY

9 St. James's Road, Belfast

### DIED 27th JULY, 1971

Aged 47 years

R.I.P.

What he suffered he told but few,
He did not deserve what he went through;
Tired and weary he made no fuss,
But tried so hard to stay with us.

Two tired eyes are sleeping,
Two willing hands are still,
The one who worked so hard for us
Is resting at God's will.

IRISH NEWS, LTD.

More frequently in his early seasons, Charlie Tully was fielded at inside-left, where he would be marked – sometimes literally – by the likes of Anderson (Aberdeen), Buchanan (Hibernian), Campbell (Morton), Cowie (Dundee), Cox (Rangers), Davidson (Partick Thistle), Gallacher (Dundee), McColl (Rangers), Mooney (Third Lanark), Philp (East Fife) and Young (Raith Rovers). It was a more physical game then, vastly different from nowadays: tackles were hard and jarring, shoulder-charging was an accepted part of the game and players could be tackled from behind with impunity. On slick, muddy pitches, the sliding tackle was the defender's art form. The hero of *From Scenes Like These* admitted:

*He'd never really liked Rangers, although he was a Protestant. Celtic had always seemed more friendly, somehow. Look at Charlie Tully. Rangers went in for strength, like granite. Charlie Tully had bowly legs and was bald and didn't look strong enough to beat carpets yet he had more personality in his little finger than Rangers had in their whole team. Charlie Tully would jink towards the Rangers defence – you'd need guts to take on big Geordie Young and Willie Woodburn and Sammy Cox and Jock Tiger Shaw – and when they came at him, ready to hammer him into the ground, he'd bamboozle them, pointing the way he pretended to pass the ball, sending them chasing in the wrong direction, or running on without the ball but still pretending to dribble so cleverly they'd follow him, trying to make a tackle.*

Referees were vastly tolerant of this physical approach – their mantra was 'It's a man's game, after all.' Gradual developments, with exposure to the game as played elsewhere, did much to protect the ball-players later and met with the approval – typically forthright – of Brian Clough: 'Some good has come out of it. We are allowing players to play who were once too frightened to walk down the tunnel because they knew they were going to get a clattering. Now they can run all over the place thinking "No bugger can kick me now."' His words remind me of an excerpt from a match report from 1949, in which the reporter reveals his own idealistic approach to the game: 'In recent weeks I have seen Jimmy Mason (Third Lanark), Gordon Smith (Hibernian) and Charlie Tully (Celtic) stopped by fouls after their footwork had beaten opponents. No doubt a defender does not relish proof that he is beatable but that hardly justifies a tackle which robs the spectator of the quota of entertainment he is usually allowed for his 1/6d (7.9p)' (*Evening Citizen*).

After the tactical success of England in the 1966 World Cup, wingers became an endangered species, unlike the heady days of the 1950s when they were an integral component of the W formation. Then it was the winger's task to hug the touchline and wait to be fed, and the inside-forward could make or break a winger with the quality of his service. For some strange reason, left-wingers were much rarer than right-wingers and were a prized possession.

Charlie Tully, given his physique and lack of genuine speed, relied on skill and cunning to open up defences with neat dribbling and intelligent distribution. In this respect he was similar to other Scottish wingers, such as Johnny Aitkenhead (Motherwell) and Charlie Johnstone (Queen of the South) – small men who could shuffle past full-backs with deceptive ease.

Some wingers were speed-merchants and could outpace the defending full-backs if they could get clear of the initial, heavy challenge. Men like Johnny Hather (Aberdeen), Jimmy Walker (Partick Thistle) and Gerry Burrell (St Mirren) – all as lean as greyhounds – fitted into this category. Others like Hibernian's Willie Ormond and a young Lawrie Reilly added goalscoring to the supplying of chances for other forwards, while the Polish pair of Alfie Lesz (St Mirren) and Felix Staroscik (Third Lanark) added the odd unexpected continental manoeuvre to their play. Willie Waddell (Rangers), Johnny Duncan (East Fife) and Ken Dawson (Falkirk) provided power, strong running and powerful finishing to their wing duties, while Eddie Rutherford (Rangers), Johnny McKenzie (Partick Thistle) and Gordon Smith – all less powerful than the previous three mentioned – were wingers in the classic Scottish mould.

One other winger deserves mention – Bobby Mitchell (Third Lanark and Newcastle United). He played on the left and was entirely unpredictable and sometimes accused of inconsistency, but no winger was ever better on his game. He must have developed a greater consistency at St James' Park, where he is still revered as 'a Geordie' and considered the equal of Stanley Matthews.

According to Sean Fallon, the long-time Celtic stalwart, 'Charlie Tully loved playing against Rangers.' Some revisionists would suggest it was because Charlie was a Catholic boy, born and brought up near the Falls Road in a bitterly divided city in Northern Ireland. The truth is probably much more simple: Tully was a player who thrived on excitement and the thrill of the big game, and few matches in world football can equal the Old Firm clashes for intensity. For Tully, it was an opportunity to test himself against the best possible opposition. When he joined Celtic, Rangers were the predominant club and Celtic – at least since the late 1930s – were always the underdogs. Johnny Paton (Tully's partner during the Irishman's first season) repeats that refrain: 'I came back to Celtic from Chelsea in the 1947–48 season. We were a young, inexperienced side and playing against a very strong Rangers team with Scottish internationals like Bobby Brown, George Young, 'Tiger' Shaw, Willie Woodburn, Ian McColl, Willie Waddell and Adam Little...'

Sean Fallon insisted that Charlie Tully's enjoyment of Old Firm clashes was due to his love of spectacle: 'He was a big-game player, and the Old Firm matches were always the biggest in Scotland. Have you noticed how often Charlie did really well on the bigger stages?' Fallon also pointed out that Old Firm players had a great deal in common, more than with the players of other clubs, in that they were frequently in the limelight on and off the pitch: 'We could understand what the other lot were going through, and sometimes that created a bond between us. I was friends with quite a few Rangers players – and so was Charlie.'

Fallon went on to tell his story of being invited along to the Plaza Ballroom on a Saturday night by George Young, Rangers' captain. Sean joined a group of Rangers players such as Young, Ian McColl and Sammy Cox along with their wives or girlfriends. At the table, Sean was soon in a whispered conversation with George Young: 'Sean, my leg is a bit sore from today's match. Could I ask you to dance with my girlfriend? I'd really appreciate it.' Young Fallon, who fancied himself as a dancer, was only too eager to agree but quickly realised that McColl and Cox were approaching him with much the same request. 'I was up on the floor all night dancing with their girlfriends, and they were sitting back drinking beer! I wasn't complaining; I didn't drink in those days, and they were all pretty girls.' He continued with his recollection:

> George Young – 'Corky' we called him – was a great fellow, a lovely man. As captain of Rangers (and Scotland), he had a lot of contacts. And he would often get a lot of players – Celtic's included – wee part-time jobs. I remember he got some of us to turn up at a clothing shop on Renfield Street a couple of afternoons a week. All we had to do was to be there, talk to some of the customers and the owner would give us three or four pounds for our trouble. The money came in very handy, because we didn't get too much in those days. Charlie, of course, was always a star turn on those occasions; he loved meeting and talking to people.

Speaking of George Young (often Rangers' right-back and Charlie Tully's immediate opponent) reminded Fallon that it was the Ranger who had nominated him as a member of Pollok Golf Club back in the 1950s – 'and I'm still a member today.' He was pleased to expand on the friendly relations. 'Back in the 1950s Old Firm players could meet socially without any hassle. We could go out for a meal and, even though we were noticed, we were left alone. Charlie was a sociable type and he had friends everywhere, even at Ibrox. He never had any time for fighting about religion.'

After the home international match (1–1) between Scotland and Northern Ireland at Hampden Park on 5 November 1952, Charlie Tully and George Young exchanged jerseys at the end. As always, the pair had played each other amicably. Presumably, it was only another sporting gesture, as it is unlikely that the diminutive Tully and the giant Young would have fitted each other's jerseys. Even more surprisingly, relations between the Celtic Supporters' Association and Rangers were cordial, and several players were frequent and well-received guests at CSC rallies. These included 'Tiger' Shaw, Willie Woodburn and George Young – all of whom would be considered uncompromising opponents on the field.

Similarly, Sean Fallon – even after more than 50 years in Glasgow, possessed with a thick Irish accent and a face described as 'a map of Ireland' – has never had any problems with any possible sectarian divide. 'When I played for the Irish League (Northern Ireland), I didn't know what religion they were although most of them would have been Protestants. You could never have met nicer guys.' He returned to the theme that Charlie Tully enjoyed playing against Rangers:

*He loved those games, even against Sammy Cox. Did you know that, despite that game at Ibrox, they were the best of pals? They got on very well. In those days there was a great deal of respect and liking among the players. I remember that Sammy — who came from Ayrshire, I think — used to be able to get extra supplies of meat during the rationing. Very often he used to bring in cuts of meat for me and Charlie, and they were very welcome in those days of shortages. I wish the supporters could have seen how well we got on.*

Sammy Cox verified this in a (much later) interview, speaking of the infamous 1949 match at Ibrox:

*Charlie came down to Kilmarnock to see me on the Sunday. The newspaper he wrote for contacted me and asked if it was all right if they came to take a picture. Charlie, who was a delightful bloke, sat with me and the family as if we had just had a party the day before. You wouldn't have thought we had caused a rude word, let alone a near riot. He told me afterwards that Bob Kelly had been incensed that he'd gone anywhere near me. But Charlie was a law unto himself.*

'Tiny' Wharton, the well-known and outsize referee, related that he used to give both Charlie Tully and Sammy Cox a lift into town regularly from Clarkston. And the practice continued even after the infamous Cox–Tully incident in the League Cup tie. 'They used to sit in the car and needle each other. All in good humour.' The former official also pointed out that he designated himself as T. Wharton (Clarkston) in order to get appointed for more games than he would have got had he called himself T. Wharton (Glasgow).

After the interview with Fallon, he walked me to my car, and I could see that he was anxious to provide as much information about Charlie Tully as he could. To my amusement — very much hidden, I can assure you — he insisted that Charlie Tully sat on the ball during his first Old Firm match. I did not have the heart – or the nerve – to tell him that Rangers won 1–0 in Tully's first appearance in an Old Firm game and that Charlie Tully – no matter how well he played in the next clash with Rangers – certainly did not sit on the ball.

Perhaps, in a parallel universe such as envisioned in theoretical quantum physics, Charlie Tully did sit on the ball in that game but not in mine as a reasonably objective observer. Probably Sean Fallon was playing for Glenavon in the Irish League that day (25 September 1948), but clear in his mind was the image of Charlie Tully actually sitting on the ball in the hurly-burly of an Old Firm Cup tie. It made me realise the power of myth; Tully should have sat on the ball, but I know he didn't. And, still talking at the car in the parking lot, Sean introduced me as a Celtic man writing a book about Charlie Tully to an elderly neighbour. This neighbour – a Rangers supporter, I found out shortly afterwards – scratched his head: 'Charlie Tully? I remember him well. I saw him sit on the ball in a match against Rangers at Parkhead. A great player!' Sometimes it is impossible to defeat the enduring force of myth!

Driving back to Edinburgh, I thought of Charlie Tully and Rangers. I had been fortunate to see many of those matches, and the memories flooded back:

25 September 1948, Celtic 3 Rangers 1: Charlie Tully's greatest day in a Celtic jersey, and a day to be treasured by every Celtic supporter who had seen a football genius working his magic against Rangers.

27 August 1949, Rangers 2 Celtic 0: The day that Charlie Tully was assaulted by Sammy Cox and became a martyr in some Celtic eyes.

23 September 1950, Celtic 3 Rangers 2: An evenly matched game entered the last 10 minutes with Rangers leading by 2–1, until Tully changed things. A swerving

cross caught Woodburn on the arm, and McPhail scored from the penalty spot. Three minutes later, another cross from Tully found Peacock in the clear for the winning goal.

20 September 1952, Celtic 2 Rangers 1: Celtic, with two full-backs in an improvised forward line, were determined to win this match to honour their young player John Millsop, who had been buried that morning. Celtic scored twice within the first 10 minutes, and early on, Tully executed a dazzling scissor-kick on a greasy pitch to help settle any nerves.

15 August 1956, Celtic 2 Rangers 1: This League Cup tie was delicately poised at 1–1 when Tully, facing 'The Jungle' in a crowded penalty area, gathered the ball, kept it up for a second or two and then lobbed the ball over his own head and into Rangers' net at the junction of the far post and crossbar.

19 October 1957, Celtic 7 Rangers 1: On a day when Celtic gave one of their best-ever team performances and when some Celtic players produced the game of their lives, the veteran Charlie Tully was still one of the best men on the pitch.

And what was his very first appearance against Rangers? The Royal Ulster Constabulary Sports at the Balmoral Showgrounds in Belfast was once a popular event, and Glasgow Rangers always sent a team for the five-a-sides. Charlie played for Belfast Celtic against a strong quintet from Ibrox in 1947, and he impressed observers from Celtic Park despite ending up on the losing side. A year later, he was signed and arrived in Glasgow to start his contribution to one of football's great rivalries.

And, of course, Tully was once transferred to Rangers. On 11 March 1959 an Old Firm Select went to Inverness to christen the lights at Inverness Caledonian's stadium. As SFA regulations required that all players had to belong to one club, apart from for international matches, Charlie Tully and the other Celtic players involved had to sign for Rangers for the occasion. The Old Firm Select, playing in hoops (red, white and blue ones), won by 4–2.

## Note

1. It was scarcely surprising, as the representative sides were chosen by committees often working to personal agendas. The Management Committee, consisting of 12 club directors, chose the players to represent the Scottish League; the full Scotland international team was chosen by seven SFA selectors. This goes some way to explain the baffling overlooking over the years of such performers as Jimmy McGrory (Celtic), Gordon Smith (Hibernian) and Willie McNaught (Raith Rovers).

# Chapter 15

# The End in Glasgow

On my visit to Belfast I asked about any possible unfair treatment of Charlie Tully by the Irish selectors. Malcolm Brodie, the veteran sports journalist and a great admirer of Tully, said 'Charlie was very much an individualist, a one-off. It was not always easy to fit him into a team pattern. A great pity, but he did get 10 caps.' Charlie Tully Jr confirmed 'Ten caps, he got. That wasn't too many; I often wondered about that.' Billy, Charlie's brother, also said 'Charlie Tully should have been given many more caps than he got – and you know damned well why that was the case.'

Charlie Tully was more than disappointed at being overlooked for the Northern Ireland squad for the World Cup, to be held in Sweden in the summer of 1958. According to his brother, Charlie was so incensed that he confronted Harry Cavan, the IFA secretary, about his omission.[1] If the contretemps did take place as described by Billy, it would have been one of the few times Charlie went public with his views on any institutionalised discrimination within Northern Ireland football. Allegedly Tully, in the heated confrontation with the IFA official, described the squad as 'more like Garmoyle United than Northern Ireland' – a reference to the fact that the association's headquarters was in Garmoyle Street in a predominantly Protestant area of Belfast. Actually, Northern Ireland played very well in the competition, and Celtic's Bertie Peacock was one of their stars. Tully's place in the squad was taken by Sammy McCrory of Southend United, but he did not play in any of the matches.

At the start of the 1958–59 season Tully was a regular once more in Celtic's side and played a leading part in the bid to retain the League Cup – once considered Celtic's jinx competition. He played in all eight matches in Celtic's campaign and had the distinction of scoring Celtic's first goal in the tournament – an equaliser against Clyde at Shawfield in the opening game, which paved the way for a 4–1 win.

Only two weeks later in a home game against St Mirren, he scored again in a 3–0 win. Two goals in three matches was heady going for the veteran, but those goals in August were the last he netted for Celtic. In fact, after the famous 7–1 triumph in the 1957 League Cup Final, Charlie Tully only made another 21 appearances for Celtic in the major competitions (the League, League Cup and Scottish Cup).

During that League Cup campaign Tully, still at outside-right, played well and, according to a newspaper account of the semi-final, he came close to one of his best performances: 'The winners of the Scottish League Cup for the past two seasons, Glasgow Celtic have failed in their bid to bring off the hat-trick. Before a floodlit crowd of 50,000 at Ibrox last night, they suffered a shock 2–1 defeat to Partick Thistle. Celtic have only themselves to blame, missing chance after chance. Their best player – indeed the star of the match – was none other than the veteran Charlie Tully. Tully presented his mates with enough chances to have won the match twice over' (*Belfast Telegraph*, 2 October 1958).

A couple of weeks later, Tully made his last international appearance for Northern Ireland (against Spain in the Bernabeu), but it was an unhappy occasion both for him and his team. He had been a surprise selection, recalled after a three-year absence.[2] For that match on 15 October 1958 the Spanish players were on a bonus of £250 each for winning (which they did by 6–2), while the Irishmen received only £50 a man. More than 100,000 were present at the Bernabeu, the most modern stadium in Europe and described in the contemporary newspapers as 'a cathedral of football'. The gate receipts were estimated at a little more than £25,000, all of which was retained by the Spanish FA; the 'gate' at the return match at Windsor Park would become the sole property of the Northern Ireland FA. The teams lined up as follows:

**Spain:** Alonso (Real Madrid), Quincoces (Valencia), Lesmes (Real Madrid), Sansisteban (Real Madrid), Santamaria (Real Madrid), Zarraga (Real Madrid), Tegada (Barcelona), Kubala (Barcelona), Di Stefano (Real Madrid), Suarez (Barcelona), Gento (Real Madrid).

**Northern Ireland:** Uprichard (Portsmouth), Keith (Newcastle United), McMichael (Newcastle United), Blanchflower (Tottenham Hotspur), Forde (Ards), Casey (Portsmouth), Bingham (Luton Town), Cush (Leeds United), McParland (Aston Villa), McIlroy (Burnley), Tully (Celtic).

General Franco was unable to attend the match as the 10 days' mourning period for Pope Pius XII had not ended, but the Spanish side contained no fewer than seven Real Madrid players – probably in expectation of his attendance, as Real Madrid were known to be the Spanish leader's favourite team. Disappointingly, after their gallant efforts at the World Cup in the summer, Northern Ireland were totally outplayed, and only a magnificent display by Uprichard in goal kept the score down to respectable figures (6–2). Tully, after getting a knock to his knee in the first half, was largely invisible.

After the crushing defeat, Charlie must have realised that his international career was over, but worse news awaited him in Glasgow. Word had got out that he was on the verge of signing a deal with Stanley Paul Publishing to produce his autobiography, ghostwritten by Malky Munro of the *Evening Citizen*. This was ground-breaking work, as only three previous books about Scottish football personalities had been written at that point.[3] As well as being the first autobiography by a Celtic player, the transaction would have been 'a good little earner' for Tully, but Celtic objected.

Desmond White, the club's secretary and no great admirer of Tully as a player, spoke to him almost immediately after his return from Spain. A veiled ultimatum – according to Billy – was issued, and Tully's own future career at Celtic Park would have to be reviewed. Charlie was reprimanded and reminded that a clause in his contract expressly forbade such publications. According to a copy of Tully's contract in the possession of his son, and seen by the author, the club's secretary was correct in the strict legal sense: 'The player hereby undertakes not to take part in journalism in any manner of way connected with the game or the government thereof during the subsistence of this contract.' He was also told that his first-team appearances could be curtailed and that, if he were demoted to the reserves, he would be expected to fulfil 'coaching on the pitch' with the youngsters.

The writing may have been on the wall for the player, but it seems that the publication of the autobiography was a convenient excuse for the club to start the process of releasing him. Charlie, convinced he had at least another productive year in him, was devastated at being told he was going to be let go by Celtic and made a point of contacting the chairman. Bob Kelly, inwardly sympathetic, explained it thus: 'It's time for new blood, Charlie.'[4] Carrie was bitter: 'That's what they do to you when they don't think you can give them anything else. And they don't have pension plans for football players.'

From the club's point of view, Charlie Tully, after 10 seasons with Celtic, had slowed down. He was becoming increasingly injury-prone, and his form had shaded. Where he had once been tolerated as an individualist who could transform matches with 10 minutes of brilliance, those episodes were becoming more and more infrequent. It was time for Charlie Tully to retire, gracefully if possible.

Like all players, Charlie Tully still believed he had a role to play at Celtic Park and within the first team. He could point out reasonably accurately that his football mind was as sharp as ever, that he could still exercise mastery over the ball and that these two priceless gifts could compensate for a decline in fitness and pace. The feeling persisted that Celtic were now prepared to release the player and that the publication of his memoirs was a convenient pretext; after all, the *Evening Citizen* had published a weekly column, ghostwritten for the player, for a number of years – and nobody at Celtic Park had been known ever to complain about it, with the notable exception of Bobby Evans.

The misfortune for Tully was that he played before the use of substitutes became legitimate in Scotland. Had he been used sparingly, available to come off the bench to change the pattern of a game, Charlie Tully could well have played another three seasons at the top level in Glasgow as a star player. For Shakespeare's *Hamlet,* it was much the same for Tully:

*The time is out of joint. O cursed spite*
*That ever I was born to set it right.*

Both Billy (Charlie's brother) and Charlie Jr (his son) believe and insist that the book *Passed to You* was a major factor in his leaving Celtic within a year of its publication. Billy is forthright: 'That book was the death knell for Charlie at Celtic Park,' while Charlie Jr is more realistic: 'It helped hasten my father's departure.' Certainly the chronology fits the thesis. The book came out in 1958, a couple of months before Christmas, and Charlie Tully left in 1959, having made only 15 appearances in Celtic's first team that season – and only one after November 1958.

In the *Daily Record* of 22 September 1958, James Stevenson gave a rave review of 'Celtic's old-boy right wing (Tully and Fernie) that was positively devastating' in a 3–1 win over Raith Rovers in a League fixture at Parkhead two days previously. 'Fernie in his favourite position of inside-right was the complete footballer, scoring two goals and weaving his way through the opposition with masterly control,' while Tully roasted Polland and Baxter as 'he wiggled his way out on the right wing' to create two of Celtic's goals. Sadly, it was like an Indian summer performance for the two veteran Celtic stars, but how much did the teenage Jim Baxter learn from the experience?

A week later, on 27 September 1958, Charlie Tully made his last League appearance for Celtic in a fixture against Aberdeen at Pittodrie – a lacklustre 3–1 defeat from the strong-going Dons. Four days later at Ibrox Park, he made his last appearance in the League Cup in a 2–1 semi-final defeat by Partick Thistle and, according to the newspaper reports, he was one of Celtic's better performers on the night.

It was the beginning of the end for the veteran, now having great difficulty in recovering quickly from injury. Three days after the League Cup defeat, he missed the League match against Queen of the South due to a back injury, presumably sustained against Thistle. It was an injury that lingered, because he did not feature in any Celtic first team for four months, returning on 31 January 1959 in a Scottish Cup tie against Albion Rovers, which Celtic won 4–0.

The match – perhaps in an attempt to drum up interest in a routine Cup tie – had been billed as 'a comeback game' for Charlie Tully, but it was played on a frosty Celtic Park pitch that 'lay smothered in a "beat-the-frost" blanket of sand'. Tully, who had come 'prancing into the game with vintage footwork' at the outset, went down heavily 'with a leg knock' shortly after the interval – later amended in the same newspaper *(Evening Times)* on the following Monday to 'a knee injury'. He was, however, able to complete the match, although in some discomfort. Objective observers might wonder why Celtic risked Tully's comeback on such a dodgy surface, especially after such a long absence. It seems to reflect badly on the level of professionalism in the Celtic backroom staff. John McPhail noted the 'flint surface' and commented that Tully, 'wily as ever, had a serviceable match and I am convinced he would have starred in the second half but for receiving a knee knock' (*Daily Record*, 2 February 1959). It was his last appearance in a Celtic jersey in a competitive fixture.

On 30 April 1959 Charlie Tully attended the Reserve League Cup Final between Celtic and Falkirk at Parkhead, watched by more than 10,000. Commenting on recent press speculation about his future, he told John McPhail 'I am not on Celtic's free transfer list, nor am I for sale. I will be connected with Celtic next season.' This match ended in a 2–2 draw, thus giving Falkirk the trophy on a 3–2 aggregate. Celtic's side contained four future Lisbon Lions in Billy McNeill, John Clark, Stevie Chalmers and Bertie Auld. The guard was changing at Celtic Park.

Leaving a club like Celtic after a long career must be a wrench at the best of times – but to do so in stressful circumstances? The football world is filled with tales of 'loyal servants' departing the scene, vowing never to enter the club's ground again. The image of an embittered Willie Maley at Celtic Park as player, match secretary and manager from the club's first game in 1888 until his abrupt and unwilling departure in 1940 springs immediately to mind in a Celtic context. The 70-year-old Maley apparently vowed never to come back to Celtic Park again; indeed, he was frequently observed as a guest of Rangers at Ibrox during the wartime seasons. The whole scenario was not the case with Charlie Tully. There would have been unhappiness and disappointment mingled with a sense of betrayal. But in his heart, the player must have been aware of his own decline and recognised that his career in Scotland as a star player was over.

A great deal of the rumours about Charlie Tully's future were revealed in the *Daily Record* by John McPhail, presumably relying on his long-lasting friendship with Charlie: 'There has never been any question of Charlie Tully being freed by Celtic, or placed on the transfer list. That is what Mr Bob Kelly, chairman of Celtic, told me last night but, knowing the history of Charlie's muscle injuries, Mr Kelly did not hold an optimistic view of the Irishman playing a lot of football next season. But I can assure you that, if Tully does not sport the green-and-white shirt very often, his worth will not be lost to the club. Charlie Tully, with his soccer knowledge and general popularity, could well make a first-class scout – and that could be his official capacity next season' (1 May 1959).

The fact that McPhail's confident predictions did not come true indicates there was an element of confusion at the time. Clearly, Charlie Tully was not going to be retained as a player, but some negotiations appeared to have been taking place about a future role at Celtic Park. Otherwise, why would he have attended Celtic's pre-season training?

In the *Daily Record* (14 July 1959), John McPhail reported on the start of training at Celtic Park the day before: 'Charlie trained with the Celtic players but the Irish internationalist told me that he had retired and would not play for Celtic this season.' The *Evening Times* (15 July 1959) corroborated this: 'Even Charlie Tully, complete with his usual 'toorie', appeared as fresh as paint in spite of the fact that the Irishman will play no more competitive football.'

In the end, Celtic declined to avail themselves of his services. Instead, Bob Kelly, the man who made the important decisions at Celtic Park, had long-range plans for another Irishman, Sean Fallon. One critic, noting the differences between the pair, commented that Kelly 'was opting for the tortoise rather than the hare'. Fallon went lame in the pre-season trial match in August 1958 and, despite his general fitness, was unable to recover from a chronic knee injury. The chairman would reward him for his earnest and unwavering loyalty to Celtic by appointing him as a coach, from which he later emerged as assistant manager to Jock Stein – and Charlie Tully would be free to go.

There would be compensations, of course. Carrie, for instance, would have been delighted at the prospect of returning to Belfast; the children, Charlie and Patricia, had spent all their summer holidays in Ireland and would not have felt uprooted.

Carrie was Belfast-born and bred. When she first met Charlie, she was working in a bakery in the lower Falls Road. The move to Glasgow had come as a shock to Charlie – even though he had become accustomed to a life in the limelight with Belfast Celtic – but for Carrie it would have been almost traumatic. She felt isolated in Glasgow. Living in a spacious club-owned house at 174 Randolph Drive in Clarkston was vastly different from a terraced council house in Belfast. Almost literally, until the move to Glasgow, she had never known a life other than within a close-knit Belfast community, she had rarely been anywhere else (apart from a stint working in an upmarket dress shop in the High Street, off Royal Avenue in Belfast) and she was unprepared for and naturally overwhelmed by the publicity her new husband was generating in football-mad Glasgow. While Charlie could put on his act and seem to revel in the attention, Carrie tended to withdraw. Audrey Fernie described her as 'a very quiet girl – at least here in Scotland. I saw her only at Celtic functions with Charlie'. However, it was recognised as a happy marriage, and Charlie and Carrie were friends as well as spouses. Charlie Jr remembers that they talked a lot. 'Charlie would give my mother a full account of his day describing in detail exactly what he did, what he said…and Carrie was able to offer her opinions freely; she was a typical Belfast girl in that respect.' Charlie Tully Jr adds 'It goes almost without saying that she was a very warm, loving mother – and very protective of her children.' In reality, she lived for the closed season to arrive – and for the family to leave Glasgow and head to Belfast. In Glasgow, football wives were left largely to their own devices, and often it was a lonely life for Carrie.

Charlie's ambition of managing a reborn and revived Belfast Celtic was stirring again, and a move back to Belfast would bring it closer to realisation, he hoped…but in vain. The man himself would soon have the consolation of becoming the player-manager of Cork Hibs, and at a salary reputedly higher than his previous one at Celtic Park, but it involved considerable travel to Cork from Belfast.

Back home in Belfast, money quickly became a problem and scarcely surprisingly. Many people have trouble in handling their personal finances even in more modern times, and why should Charlie Tully be different? He started off with considerable disadvantages: born into a large family in 1924 in working-class west Belfast, a member of an impoverished community, a resident of a terraced council house growing up and a school-leaver at 14 with little formal education, skilled only in one possible career. What practical training had he ever received in managing money?

## Notes

1. Harry Cavan was highly esteemed in the football world, rising to a high rank within UEFA. Previously he had been a Trades Union official and chairman of Ards. When Rangers were under a form of investigation for their 'policy' of not signing Catholic players, Cavan was chosen by UEFA to lead the inquiry. He reported that Rangers had no case to answer.
2. Charlie Tully played 10 times for Northern Ireland – and never once played on a winning side. This might reflect the generally low level attained by the national side rather than shortcomings on Tully's part. For the record, his appearances were as follows:

    *1948 – England (2–6)*
    *1949 – England (2–9)*
    *1951 – Scotland (0–3)*
    *1952 – England (2–2), Scotland (1–1), France (1–3)*
    *1953 –Wales (2–3), Scotland (1–3)*
    *1955 – England (0–3)*
    *1958 – Spain (2–6)*

3. The titles are *50 Years in Football* by Matha Gemmell (1943), *Memoirs* by Jerry Dawson (1949) and *Captain of Scotland* by George Young (1952). Matha Gemmell was the pawky trainer of Clyde and a much-loved personality in the game; Jerry Dawson was the recently retired Rangers and Scotland goalkeeper; George Young was a full-back and centre-half for both Rangers and Scotland.

4. It gave Bob Kelly an opportunity to tinker even more with matters best left to the manager. For almost seven years – a biblical span – Celtic fielded sides far too young and inexperienced to cope with the challenges of top-grade football in Scotland. Many Celtic followers became disillusioned with this youth policy, optimistically called 'the Kelly Kids'.

# Chapter 16
## *When the Cheering Stops*

On the day of his funeral, Charlie Tully's great exploits on the football pitch were recalled (and rightly so) in St John's, on the Falls Road, at his graveside and wherever Celtic-minded people gather worldwide.

Few, however, commented on the reality of a player's working life outside his playing days. His own autobiography, entertaining as it was, glossed over the hardships of those early days in the 1920s and 1930s. It has become almost mandatory for those recalling hard times to present a sentimental, romanticised account of the past. Despite the acclaim and the publicity of a career in football, there was no guarantee of a passport out of the working class in the 1950s. As Charlie Tully Jr pointed out 'My father achieved a lot of fame but that did not translate into fortune.'

Young men, poorly educated for the most part, were inclined to gamble on the continuation of a football career to the exclusion of everything else and were notoriously ill-prepared to earn a living after their years in the limelight. Few careers in football beckoned for the retiring player in the 1960s. He might be offered a job as a manager but that was mainly for the well-known, as the clubs traded on their fame or reputation to attract younger players. Coaching was still a suspect occupation, and the managers in the 1950s were expected to carry out a variety of tasks, often inside an office, so very little in a player's life would have prepared him for this admittedly unglamorous role.

More likely, the ex-player might go into the licensing trade, either as the outright owner of a pub or as a front man for a brewery. For a very long time, the pinnacle of ambition was thought to be the pub landlord of a premises near a football ground. It could be said uncharitably that a career spent in a pub hardly counted as a change of profession for some players, but the work demanded a grasp of business principles for which few were ready.

Of course, there was always journalism — that refuge of the semi-literate — but the player had to be well known, controversial or a former Ranger in Scotland, where journalism appeared to be an occupation reserved for ex-Ibrox players.

An ex-player who had spent little and saved hard, if he was lucky, could afford to set up a newsagents; others could expect unskilled work in a factory or labouring, or a life scrounging on the benefits system.

In too many cases (and even for a great player such as Charlie Tully), it was a circular journey back to the same, still impoverished neighbourhood. Any improvements in living conditions were those effected only by the passage of a decade or so, and these were minimal in the slow-moving 1950s. Most players sensed or knew they were heading back into a working-class community when their playing careers were over. Perhaps — with wages relatively low — they had never really left it, as many players still lived in the same districts alongside those who packed the terraces to watch them every week in the immediate post-war seasons.

It could be argued that a player in the 1940s and 1950s was little more than an indentured servant to a club who, for the most part, exploited him. Normally a player signed a contract that bound him to the club for a 12-month period. At the end of that time, it was the club who held all the high cards. A player was not at liberty to move elsewhere unless with the club's approval, and the club had three options: to release the player outright, to put him on the transfer list or to retain him for a further 12-month period. An average player given a free transfer might experience difficulty in finding another club, the player on the transfer list might find it hard to find a club willing to pay the valuation put on him and a player retained by his current club could find that his wages or bonuses had been set by the club.

The only 'option' for a player was to refuse to agree to the new terms offered, but a refusal meant he was retained but paid no wages. As the club held his registration, the player could not play elsewhere.

The one exception was that a player could sign on for non-League clubs, who were not bound by the salary scale that League clubs had agreed in order to curtail the free movement of players. Jock Stein left Albion Rovers to join Llanelly, as did Dougie Wallace of Clyde. Even more bizarre was the mini-exodus of British players to Colombia in the 1940s; Colombia was not a member of FIFA and thus not bound by regulations involving transfers.

Equally discriminatory was the cap on players' wages decided upon by the League clubs. It was an arrangement by which all players, no matter how talented, could not receive any money beyond the limit set by the clubs. Thus, it was theoretically possible that a journeyman player for Celtic could be earning the same amount of money as Charlie Tully, whose appearance in the side had probably added thousands of spectators to the gate. Workers in no other industry worked under such restrictions.

Even the bait of living in a club house proved yet another means of ensuring player compliance. The player had only 12 months of security and, unused to dealing with banks or mortgage companies, was reluctant or afraid to purchase a house of his own. A mortgage in the more unsophisticated era of the 1950s carried the stigma (or suggestion) of debt for many, and a player, at the mercy of his club, had to think very carefully before entering into a 25-year agreement with a bank. It was safer to remain in a club house and pay the rent to the club.

Charlie Tully Jr still has a copy of his father's contract for 1955. Tully was offered £14 a week and £11 in the closed season. He could increase his salary by gaining a bonus of £1 a point, but that potential increase of 14.28 per cent was possible only if he were a member of the side that gained full points. If he were out of the team through loss of form, injury or suspension (or at the whim of an unpredictable chairman), he was not eligible for such a bonus.

Even for such a stellar performer as Tully, anxiety increased as the end of the season approached. Virtually no player was safe, especially one approaching his thirties – the traditional retirement age for most players. Football, as a business, had established its own modus operandi – and it is easy to see from a modern perspective how vulnerable it could have been to a legal challenge. However, most players – even the legends of the game – were relatively unsophisticated and cared more for playing as long as possible. Many assumed that a player such as Tully would have received preferential treatment from Celtic, but the former Celtic director Jimmy Farrell was at pains to dispel that thought: 'Desmond White (the club's secretary) was an accountant by profession, and he was in charge of all money matters. To put it bluntly, Desmond did not approve of Charlie Tully as a professional player, and he would never have given him a penny more than his contract allowed.'

At the end of the 1958–59 season Charlie Tully was released on a free transfer, having been missing from Celtic's regular line up for most of that season. A free transfer was yet another way a club could save money and possibly reward a veteran player at the same time. Free of any contractual obligations, the player was able to negotiate his own terms with any other club that was interested in him. Thus, Tully was able to work out a deal with Cork Hibs. As far as Charlie Tully Jr knows, his father was not given a benefit by Celtic after his decade of service.

Tully was upset at ending his Celtic career. Like most players he felt he had at least one more season in his ageing legs, and some authorities would agree with him. Billy McNeill is adamant:

*Charlie could play in every forward position — except for centre-forward because of the physical demands. I consider his best position would be as a winger or wide player, even though he was on the slow side. He had football intelligence and could inflict harm — but not with pace. He could hold the ball, shielding it from defenders; he knew when to pass it to better-placed players and could switch the play in a flash to keep defences off balance. Defenders are always afraid of the unexpected, and they gave Charlie a lot of room — and that was what he thrived on. And remember that I saw him only when he was a veteran and slowed by age.*

A little more than a month after the 7–1 game (19 October 1957), Charlie Tully suffered a muscle injury in a 5–2 win over Airdrie at Broomfield, where he was given an unsolicited compliment by a distinguished visitor, Juan Schiaffino, the legendary Uruguayan inside-forward:[1] 'With one good leg, he still made many fine moves and clever passes. If he is out injured for long, Celtic will miss his presence.' Schiaffino, by now a naturalised Italian, could be considered an objective expert witness. He had been devastating in Uruguay's 7–0 rout of Scotland in the 1954 World Cup in Switzerland, and he had just helped AC Milan romp to a 4–1 victory over Rangers in the European Cup the previous Wednesday. He had attended the League fixture because he was staying over in Scotland prior to joining the Italian team for a friendly against Northern Ireland in Belfast.

Charlie Tully Jr recognises his father had little idea about saving for a rainy day. 'Something'll turn up' had always been his optimistic motto, but that led to Charlie,

Carrie, Charles and Patricia having to move in with Carrie's mother and her aunt at 9 St James Road, just off the Falls Road, after leaving Glasgow. Charlie Jr admits that it was a down-sizing. 'It was a step or two up from McDonnell Street, though. It was a terraced house and very crowded, but it did have an inside toilet and bathroom – even a front parlour. Carrie's father had been a part-time bookie or a runner and gambled a bit as well. But he did have periods of relative prosperity.' He thought a bit more and shook his head. 'We all hoped it was going to be a temporary arrangement, but it became permanent the way things worked out. Shortly before he died I remember him being totally amazed at the salaries players were getting; it was about £60 a week then, I believe. I don't know what he would have said about today's rewards.'

Patricia Conlon, Charlie Tully's daughter, has a slightly different perspective: 'As children, we never really wanted for anything; there were presents for everybody at Christmas, including all the relatives. Whatever Charlie got, he handed over to Carrie. For a long time the Tully home on St James Road was the only house on the street with a telephone. All the neighbours felt free to drop in to ask to use it.'

Charlie Tully – as everybody who knew him admits freely – never thought much about a future beyond football. His brother is understandably bitter: 'Charlie got good money for those days for playing football. And it's the same old story. You've always got lots of friends when you've got money. Where are those friends when you're a bit short? If all the people Charlie gave money to had paid him back, he would have been a wealthy man.'

It was only after Charlie's sudden death that the realisation grew about the precarious nature of the family's finances. Carrie was absolutely devastated at losing Charlie, becoming very quiet and withdrawn. She remained a devoted mother, especially to Brian, who was just 10 at the time. Then in her mid-40s, she had to find a job to get by. Typically, the Celtic supporters rallied round, and a Charlie Tully Memorial Fund was opened in Glasgow and raised a few thousand pounds. The cheque was presented to Carrie in Glasgow by Desmond White and Jock Stein. The manager admitted 'It's not very much but we'd like you to have it.'

A year prior to leaving Celtic, Charlie Tully had surprised some people with the assertion in his book that he was interested in becoming a manager after his playing days had ended — and he was confident about his chances of success:

*I suppose you've all got your dreams and ambitions. Well, you know mine now. To become a successful manager of a successful club...I've seen so many managers who make no attempt to get acquainted. By getting acquainted I don't mean getting familiar...as long as I was fit enough, I'd get out on the field with my players. That way you really see what's going on...First rule I'd make is that every player on my books would have a ball all to himself with his name printed on it. He'd get this ball all to himself to dribble, juggle, kick around the field. Every player would have to master that ball or I'd know why not.'*

That seems a thoroughly modern approach, written in 1958, and it was put into practice with his clubs in Ireland. The first post he took up after leaving Celtic was as player-manager and coach of Cork Hibs in the Republic of Ireland. According to his brother, his working conditions were arduous: 'The money was good, but Charlie had to travel for the games to Cork at the weekends in a Morris Minor, and that was a long way. I'm not too surprised that his legs went.' However, in his first season in charge he took them to the Final of the Football Association of Ireland Cup but lost to Shelbourne at Dalymount Park in Dublin.

'Celtic toured Ireland one pre-season, and we caught up with Charlie when he was with Cork Hibs. He was still the same jaunty personality, but no longer a great player; wonderful touches, but he could no longer last a full game,' adds Billy McNeill. Sadly he was no longer playing in an environment that matched his talent.

Charlie Tully would make one last appearance in Scotland as a competitive player at Celtic Park when he played for the League of Ireland against the Scottish League.[2] A splendid crowd of 23,500, much more than normal and most drawn by the chance to see the legendary ex-Celt in action one more time, turned up for the occasion. It was another reminder that it was the players or the performers who attracted the crowds to pay hard cash at the turnstiles.

Tully's career as a manager could not be described as a brilliant one; perhaps working in a relative backwater of football, north or south of the border, did not stimulate him sufficiently. Psychologically, it must have been a shade deflating for Charlie Tully after Glasgow. At one night game against Glentoran, Malcolm Brodie bumped into Charlie (at the time Bangor's manager) at half-time and remarked cheerfully 'Good crowd tonight, Charlie!' Tully claimed to be unimpressed: 'Malcolm, I've seen bigger crowds at half-time in the toilets at Celtic Park.' The same reliable witness attested to Charlie Tully's capabilities later, after his return to Belfast:

> Charlie was a success with Bangor as a manager. I used to meet him every Monday morning at the Rio Café near St Patrick's Church and we discussed football. Unlike many star players, he knew and appreciated every aspect of the game, the players, the tactics. He let his teams express themselves to provide entertainment, and that's scarcely a bad thing. In those sessions with me, he was a fantastic raconteur; he could hold you spellbound.

Brodie also reminded me of Tully's appearance in Glasgow: 'Charlie Tully was also the manager for the Irish League for a match against the Scottish League at Ibrox – and that has to be an indication of his ability. When the Irish party arrived in Glasgow, Charlie himself was the centre of attention.'

Charlie Tully Jr insists that his father worked hard at being a manager: 'As a manager he was a bit of a surprise. He became an early riser and was quite disciplined. He had always been highly competitive as a player, and he stayed that way as a manager…but in football terms he was always a realist.'

Padraig Coyle, a journalist and author of a history of Belfast Celtic, agrees with that last point: 'He knew he had to work within financial restraints in Northern Ireland, and many young players signed for Bangor and Portadown only because of the opportunity to work with Charlie Tully. Everybody loved Charlie, and at times there was not the essential gap between him and his players. He was conditioned to being "one of the boys".'

To summarise his managerial career: player-manager and coach of Cork Hibs in 1959, manager of Bangor from January 1964 to May 1965, manager of Portadown in 1965 and 1966, and a return to Bangor for 1967–68. His stewardship of Portadown, according to his brother Billy, was not the happiest of times. Portadown, adjoining predominantly to Catholic Lurgan, could be described as a loyalist stronghold and has been the flashpoint of recurring skirmishes during the Marching Season. Billy claims that Charlie was released shortly after photographs appeared in Belfast newspapers showing Tully at a rally alongside the moderate Gerry Fitt, by most accounts an admirable politician.

Patricia Conlon reminds me that her father always remained active in football, even after his retirement as a manager. 'He used to run a team for disadvantaged children in west Belfast, and they were not all kids with potential in football. One deaf-mute child, now an adult, occasionally runs into me in Belfast and always greets me with praise for my dad – in sign language.' She adds 'He used to take car-loads of children out to the beach at Bangor and play football there. He loved the game.' Similarly, Charlie Jr remembers that his father would watch any game of football on any public park in Belfast: 'He would go out if the weather was fine and take Brian with him to watch junior games, juvenile games, any sort of game at all. Football was in his blood.' But, year after year, the dream of a reborn Belfast Celtic, and his place within it, was receding.

In 1958 – approaching the end of his career in Scotland, when indications of financial reality could have been dawning – Tully claimed in his book that no player at Celtic Park was a member of the Scottish Players' Union, and he appeared to regret that situation. The obvious reason was that working conditions at Celtic Park and Ibrox were superior to those at other clubs. The probability of regular bonuses (at least at Ibrox) was consistently high, and the lure of turning out for either Rangers or Celtic was hard to resist. Of course, neither Old Firm club wanted any interference from a trade union in running its affairs, with both Rangers and Celtic preferring to operate on a form of paternalism. What this meant for Charlie Tully (a man not skilled in planning ahead financially) was that he was short of advice in providing for his future. A strong trade union could have provided this; a competent agent, as is the case with modern players, was simply not an option in 1959. Given the normally high attrition rate among footballers, it should have been a matter of conscience to the clubs to provide such help.

Tully was not a worldly man with money, and he appeared incapable of manipulating a situation to his own financial benefit. As a young man, he wanted to play football, loved to play for Celtic and was willing to do so at the going rate. A contemporary of Tully's, when moving to England to join a First Division outfit, was able to sell his car – recently acquired for £250 – to a director of his new club for £3,000. Charlie was never capable of such fiscal sleight of hand.

For many decades, football – the primary sport of the working class in Britain – was filled with the tragic tales of those whose careers were filled with brilliance and whose subsequent years were lived out in a degree of financial difficulty and obscurity. In that respect, Charlie Tully's life was more akin to those of Jim Baxter and Jimmy Johnstone (than to Kenny Dalglish and Alex Ferguson).

Like Baxter and Johnstone, he was a paradigm of improvidence – and almost wilfully so, giving in to the present at the expense of the future. Often the more successful sportsmen have to move onward and upward for social reasons, and this can be resented by others as a form of treason. It was a charge that could never be levelled at Jimmy Johnstone or Charlie Tully in Glasgow or Belfast. It was in one sense admirable, as it involved an almost conscious determination never to abandon one's origins – a desire to remain rooted in a familiar reality: Jimmy Johnstone drinking with old pals in Hamilton after his playing days, and Charlie Tully drinking in Falls Road pubs with his.

However, Tully's drinking was more social than an illness, differing considerably from his fellow Belfast boy George Best who, it became clear, had slipped into alcoholism. Certainly, Charlie Tully drank more than he should have, but it was within the context of nights at the pub with his friends. Billy Tully told me 'Jackie Vernon and Charlie would meet up at The Fort, a pub in Springfield Road near the Falls Road, and they would talk football all night. Totally absorbed by it, they were. Quite often the bell would ring at my house late on a Saturday night, and it would be Charlie ready to talk football well into Sunday morning.'

He may have been the first of the 'celebrity' players but, unlike the likes of Paul Gascoigne, there were no reported incidents of drunkenness, no shameful episodes of violence and no scandal, on or off the field. Sadly – at least for a biographer – it has to be admitted that the most controversial thing Charlie Tully did off-field and in public was to wear a bow tie. He probably could have made a fortune today for 'exclusive' interviews with tabloid newspapers; and, being Charlie, he would have had the native wit to make up 'suitable' scoops.

Such adherence to the past, however, as a philosophy is deeply tinged with fatalism. Football (and boxing) can be viewed as a ladder to success, but the career, no matter how glittering, ends all too soon for most – even the most famous. In some tragic cases, the downward spiral is almost self-willed and self-fulfilling. It is as if the 'failure' at the end is inevitable and to be accepted without too much of a struggle. While football can be a highly satisfying form of self-expression, fame (and security) can be transient; a career in football is pitifully short, and within 10 years the successful player can develop from 'a hopeful teenager' into 'a regular' and then into 'a veteran'. Few professions, after all, consider that a man of 30 is 'old'. With retirement, adulation fades, and a player's skill and talent no longer have a monetary value in the market place. After all, the public does not owe an ex-player a living.

However, the structure of organised football itself must bear some of the responsibility for such tragedies. Consider the situation in the 1960s. By the age of 22 almost 80 per cent of those signed up by a senior club had already dropped out of football. Charlie Tully, like many other footballers, was a victim of his times.

The system was virtually feudal and even the stars – men who deserve the status of legends within the sport – accepted the status quo. Contemporaries of Charlie Tully such as Stanley Matthews, Tom Finney and Nat Lofthouse (all of whom appeared for England against Northern Ireland during Tully's time) are recalled as exemplary figures. By displaying their extraordinary skill, they gave pleasure to thousands, more often than not in ordinary League fixtures. Quiet, retiring men, they concentrated on doing and not on talking and were private people in a way that no longer seems possible for a star player. For the showcase international matches, these players had to travel second class (apparently without too much complaint) and were paid honoraria between £20 and £50.

Derek Dougan, another Ulsterman and later a director of the PFA, railed at what he termed 'institutionalised feudalism':

*Managers are professionals at the mercy of directors who are amateurs. It seems to me to be palpably absurd that men who are supposed to know the game inside out and be devoted to it should be hired and fired by boards of directors whose real business might range from house building to pork butchering. A manager is considered an underling, a mere lackey...players are treated like serfs and paid slave wages. After retiring, they could be dumped on the scrap heap.*

In 1952 – almost in the middle of Charlie Tully's career with Celtic – a committee of investigation was brought into being by the Ministry of Labour to examine the football industry. The PFA (in England) wanted changes, but the Football League and Football Association were united in protesting that any change 'would not be in the interest of the game'. At the end of the day, the committee agreed with the authorities, pointing out that the abolition of a maximum wage would mean that richer clubs could attract better players and, accordingly, there would be little or no competition in the game.

Given the clubs' Victorian 'upstairs–downstairs' attitude towards their 'servants' (and footballers were often described in that exact term), it was not too surprising Charlie

Tully remained unskilled in money management, and his glittering career in Glasgow had not helped much. His wages from football were certainly above those of the average working man, and he could supplement his income with a ghostwritten column in an evening paper, but these careers only helped to shelter him from the reality of life as a simple wage earner. When the cheering stops, yesterday's hero quickly becomes today's forgotten man.[3]

* * *

Billy Tully, Charlie's brother, was 12 years younger than the player, and he idolised him. Understandably, he was – and remains – bitter about his brother's early death. Charlie Jr had suggested I speak to Billy: 'He knows everything about him. I'd better phone him first as he can be difficult at times.' I sat in the living room finishing my cup of tea, half listening to one end of the conversation, and judged that Billy Tully was not in the best of health but that he had agreed to see me that night.

Charlie Jr gave me more advice: 'He lives in Whiterock Road right beside the cemetery, and you'd better take a taxi there and back. It can be awkward there at times.' He thinks a bit more and adds, half-chuckling, 'Billy? You'll have to take him as you find him. He's a rough diamond and...' He stops, searching for the exact phrase and finally produces a gem. 'Tom, just remember Tullys can be odd.'

At about eight that night, after a taxi ride through a semi-deserted Falls Road, I met Billy Tully, a man in his mid-sixties. His face looked worn, and I enquired about his health; he shrugged it off but offered the information that he was going into hospital for what he described as a minor operation for a long-standing condition. Immediately, I noticed he talked very quickly, and his Belfast accent was almost impossible for me to decipher at first hearing, although the occasional expletive had a familiar ring.

He lived alone, Billy, and the house had a neglected air to it. I struggled to remember what his nephew told me. Is Billy separated, or is he a widower? The living room was determinedly masculine and filled with football memorabilia, including Celtic programmes on the table and framed football photographs on the walls – and I examine one of Belfast Celtic dated 1946–1947. Feeling I had to pass some form of test to compensate for my Scottish accent, I attempted to present my credentials: 'Charlie looks awfully young in this picture.' He agreed readily enough, adding 'He was a player even then.' 'Jackie Vernon? He was the centre-half, wasn't he?' I asked, and he confirmed: 'A great centre-half was Jackie; he played for the Great Britain team against Europe.' 'He was with West Bromwich Albion by then?' I asked. A slight relaxation on Billy's part: 'That's right. He was out with Charlie the night before he died. They were always great pals, them two.'

The international language of football talk had helped to break the ice. At least he knew now that I had heard about Belfast Celtic. Wondering how many other homes in the Falls Road still had shrines to a football club defunct since 1949, I continued 'Jimmy Jones. The one who broke his leg – ' ' – No, he had his bloody leg broken for him. The boy never played again,'[4] a touch of anger in Billy's voice here, righteous rage against the injustices of 1949. 'That was the straw that broke the back of Belfast Celtic,' he added. I nodded agreement but he paid little attention as he went into what he must have repeated hundreds of times: 'Charlie's greatest ambition was to become manager of Belfast Celtic – a born-again Belfast Celtic. He was truly heartbroken that the club was never revived.' I thought back to what Malcolm Brodie had told me a day previously:

*When Belfast Celtic disbanded in 1949 – and one of their last exploits was to beat the full Scotland international team by 2–0 in New York – it left a void in football in this country that has never been filled. There have been attempts to revive the club (and even Linfield, their greatest rivals, were involved in those efforts), but they come to nothing. Sadly, I have to think that the moment has passed now.*

Billy seemed belligerent, uncomfortably so at times, but soon it became clear that it was the argumentative certainty of the working class, where emphasis compensates for accuracy. I was very familiar with this from travelling regularly to Celtic Park on a supporters' bus; within the bluster lies more than a kernel of truth and perception. I sensed the pent-up frustration at the hurt of losing a well-loved brother at such an early age. 'Charlie died too young, far too young. It didn't seem right,' he commented bitterly. More than 30 years later, he did not seem to have come to terms with that fact.

Charlie Tully's sudden death at the age of 47 in his native Belfast may have come as a shock to the football community, but his brother Billy claimed to be not too surprised:

*His last job (as a rep for a liquor firm) was the death of him. Sometimes I think he was his own best customer. At any rate he still used to go up to the old Celtic Park and kick a ball round, but one of his friends – a Dr McGarry – noticed him often holding his chest. He spoke to him about it and finally got him to come into his surgery for a check-up. He told Charlie outright that he had angina. But Charlie just shrugged it off, as he always did. He wouldn't cut down on his drinking, and he wouldn't watch his weight; he wasn't going to change his lifestyle. He always lived as if there was no tomorrow – and one day there wasn't...*

*Well, one Monday night Charlie came home and was in the kitchen when he called out to Carrie to turn the television on; he was anxious to find out if there had been any more bombings that day.[5] Carrie had just done so when she heard a thud from the other room. She rushed back in and found Charlie on the floor almost unconscious. A massive heart attack, it was. Carrie screamed out for somebody to fetch Dr Coyne, who was a neighbour. He came rushing over, but there was nothing he could do except cradle Charlie as he died. He had to pronounce Charlie as dead later and told Carrie that the heart attack and stroke had been so massive that Charlie never had a chance to survive. He might have been trying to console Carrie when he told her that Charlie's life, had he managed to survive the attack, would have been terrible. 'Just like a vegetable,' he said. Perhaps we were lucky that Charlie was spared that.*

Billy expanded on the job as a rep for a liquor firm and the part it had played in his brother's decline.[6] 'You might find this hard to believe but he probably got more orders from the Shankill Road than from the Falls Road. It was a legacy from the hey-day of the Gaelic Association's opposition to football, which they considered a British and foreign sport. And another thing — when he died there were a lot of wreaths from Linfield and Glasgow Rangers' supporters' clubs too.'

Billy has remained bitter, clearly upset at his brother's worsening financial position after the return to Belfast. 'He got decent money when he was with Celtic, but he never saved a penny. He used to hand out money to anybody with a hard-luck story. His own father was always on to him to buy a house, but Charlie could not be bothered.' A long pause before he continued 'Hard to believe but Charlie Tully never owned a house in his life. For a long time before his death, Charlie and Carrie were reduced to living with Carrie's mother just off the Falls Road — and he was drinking more than he should by then. It's bad enough going home drunk to a wife, but to your mother-in-law as well...'

Billy went on to explain further, and it was obvious that he had related this story many times: 'Charlie left Glasgow Celtic in 1959, and he and the family returned to Belfast. Despite all his talent and 10 years with Celtic, Charlie Tully was skint.' He interrupted his train of thought to contemplate the inflated salaries of modern players, getting as much in a week as Charlie Tully earned in his entire career. 'What would he be worth today, do you think?'

Clearly, resentment lingered on Charlie Tully's behalf that he had been born into the wrong era – a common reaction among contemporaries of star players whose salaries were only marginally higher than those for skilled workers. He continued 'Charlie was very happy in Scotland and could have settled there comfortably, but Carrie wasn't. She could hardly wait to be back in Belfast near her family – and Charlie agreed to come back. But I know for a fact that his dream here was for Belfast Celtic to reopen, and he yearned to be its manager. And why not?'

It was a fair question, and I had to think about it. Tully was a star player but very much an individualist. He was a professional athlete but avoided the regimen of training like the plague…Would he have had the self-discipline necessary for a manager?[7]

Billy answered his own question: 'Well, he did well at Bangor – and had them playing decent football. Not top drawer, but entertaining. Did you know he was also manager of Pórtadown? And, when he was there, they beat Linfield in the Cup. That was some upset, let me tell you. A great night.' It was the unmistakeable voice of a man who has supported Belfast Celtic all his life. He shook his head:

> Once again, Charlie was his own worst enemy; he didn't have a contract there, and they eased him out. Well, Charlie was never a bigoted man. He would pick anybody regardless of what they were. This did not sit too well with some people

*there — and he was observed at a rally to support Gerry Fitt. His days were numbered after that. But can you imagine taking on a job like that and without a written contract? Imagine not having the sense to insist on a contract! He would have got something out of it — and he should have.*

He shook his head again: 'That was Charlie.'

## Notes

1. When I first heard this story, I assumed it was apocryphal — one of the many that helped to create the myth of Charlie Tully. However, Pat Woods (who recounted it in the excellent *Oh, Hampden in the Sun*) assures me it is true and added that a picture of Schiaffino in the Broomfield Stand appeared in the *Scottish Sunday Express* of 1 December 1957. Pat generously sent me his file and the clippings for me to verify for myself.

2. Charlie Tully made his very last appearance as a player on Scottish soil was in excellent company. The Ford Motor Company sponsored an invitational five-a-side competition at Meadowbank Sports Centre in Edinburgh on 10 February 1971, and only veteran ex-players were extended an invite for squads representing Scotland, England, Ireland, Wales, Europe A and Europe B. Turning out for Scotland were players such as George Farm (Hibernian), Willie Fernie (Celtic), Willie Woodburn (Rangers) and Graham Leggatt (Aberdeen); for England, Stanley Matthews (Blackpool), Tom Finney (Preston), Billy Wright (Wolverhampton) and Nat Lofthouse (Bolton); John Charles represented Wales and Sammy McIlroy Ireland, while among those appearing for Europe were Kubala (Spain), Fontaine (France) and Hidegkuti (Hungary). The football was secondary, the event being a last chance to pay homage to world-class footballers in a gathering described in *The Scotsman* (11 February 1971) as 'a Klondyke for Autographs'. Charlie Tully was 46 years old at the time.

3. Bertie Peacock, Charlie's teammate with Celtic and Northern Ireland for several years, is a notable exception. As a player, he was outstanding either as left-half, inside-left or outside-left; as a captain, he was encouraging and inspiring, but his life did not stop after his retirement as a player. He was a credit to himself in every possible way, and a genuine role model for everybody in his community, especially in Coleraine. There, he worked as a player, coach, manager, director and chairman. As Northern Ireland's manager for five years, he gave both Pat Jennings and George Best their international debuts in 1962. Latterly, he was also very active with the Coleraine Sports Council, in which capacity he initiated the Milk Cup — a competition designed to provide a theatre for youth teams from different countries. A lovely man!

4. Not exactly true. Jimmy Jones was out of the game for more than a year, by which time Belfast Celtic had disbanded. He played briefly for Fulham, Larne and Glenavon. In fact, he won three caps for Northern Ireland in 1956–57 when playing for Glenavon.

5. Billy's recollection is accurate: on Monday 26 July 1971 there were explosions in Belfast where the Northern Ireland Youth Employment Services were based. Branches of the Northern Bank and Belfast Co-operative were also damaged. No one was reported injured. Nine police were injured,

some seriously, in crowd trouble following a Gaelic football match at Casement Park in the Upper Falls Road. The trouble was precipitated by a traffic jam as the crowd left the stadium.

6. The company Charlie worked for was G. McShane & Co, a family owned business based in Madrid Street, east Belfast, and anxious to expand its territory. Charlie was employed to visit pubs and clubs in west Belfast to encourage them to switch their business to his company.

7. I had been thinking of Charlie Tully as I remembered him – as a brilliant player for Celtic. At this point in my research, his early days with Belfast Celtic and his subsequent career with Cork Hibs, Bangor and Portadown remained uncharted territory.

# Chapter 17
## *The Road All Runners Come*

On 31 July 1971 John Rafferty, the football correspondent for *The Scotsman*, started a series titled 'The Decline and Fall of Scottish Football'. Despite the fact that Celtic had reached the European Cup Final of 1970 – and indeed had recently played a 1–1 draw in Glasgow against their conquerors and current World Club champions Feyenoord – Rafferty argued that football was 'a declining industry, marked by dull and uninspired direction from the top, and increased sales resistance by the public'. He traced the decrease in attendances from the boom times just after World War Two to the present, pointing out that only five Scottish clubs (Aberdeen, Celtic, Hearts, Hibernian and Rangers) now had average home 'gates' above 10,000.

Elsewhere in the newspaper, he wrote about the firing of Bobby Brown – the former Rangers goalkeeper – as the Scottish manager. This position was at an evolutionary stage, with the manager still subordinate to a group of 'selectors' who were under increased pressure to appoint a full-time professional manager, but in the tradition of football, administrators were reluctant to give up any of their power. At the time, the financial rewards for being the national manager were not tempting for high-flyers, having been set at £4,000 per annum.

Rafferty, a highly respected journalist and a man who had been involved in the Scottish sports scene for many years, tied in these events with the death of Charlie Tully:

*Charlie Tully was regarded as a joker but was a man who spoke a lot of good sense. He said of the manager situation: 'I know it's a lot of power to hand over to one man, but why keep a dog and bark yourself?' ... Talking of Charles Patrick Tully made us realise what is wrong with much of the football nowadays. He was great fun, a great entertainer, a great individualist – but yet a great player, and a great team man. Celtic were in a dreadful state for some seasons after the war, and recovered only in the 1950s; there would have been no such glory without Charles Patrick... Nowadays much of the natural football would have been coached out of him. He would have been most likely made to conform – when his great gift was to terrify the opposition with the uninhibited nature of his play. Natural players such as Charlie Tully used to be the great strength of Scottish football. But now we have conformists in the main, and troublesome players are shunned instead of being coaxed with understanding.[1] Yet we have stopped winning and the crowds have lost interest... Some considered Charlie cheeky, and some others thought he was a comedian with a ball at his feet. But they should remember the day he took a corner-kick at Falkirk... Charlie Tully could do things with a ball, and that is what entertaining football is about.*

But Charlie Tully was dead, dead before his time at 47, and had been buried a few days earlier in his native Belfast. The funeral was at St John's Church and the Requiem Mass celebrated by Reverend Father Tom Hegarty, who had also officiated at the wedding of Charlie and Carrie back in 1948. They came from far and wide across the world of Irish football, and both sides of the divide in Ulster life joined in tribute to a man whose skill with a football and personality had transcended that potential for bitterness. And this was at the height of 'The Troubles', when every public occasion held the risk of terrorism.

The mourners constituted an honour guard. Firstly, all Irish League teams had sent officials and players, and the Irish Football Association was represented by its secretary, Billy Drennan. The famed Joe Bambrick, Gibby McKenzie and the Northern Ireland internationals of his time were there (Alf McMichael, Norman Uprichard, Peter McParland, Billy Humphries, Harry Creighton, Paul Murphy, Johnny Cochrane, Brian Mulgrew, Billy Bingham and Danny Trainor). The old guard of Belfast Celtic turned out in strength (Joe Douglas, Harry Walker, Norman Kernohan, Jack Ryan, Bertie Fulton, Jack Vernon, Liam Flanagan, Jimmy McAlinden, Artie

McGivern, Tommy Breen, Sean McCann, Jimmy Gallagher, Paddy Murphy and Paddy Bonnar), and Glasgow Celtic had a strong representation (Jock Stein, Jimmy Farrell, Jimmy McGrory, Sean Fallon, Johnny Bonnar and Bertie Peacock, who came along from Coleraine). Belfast Celtic FC (although defunct since 1949) sent Brendan Fitzpatrick, its secretary, and Cyril McAlinden, its director. Wreaths and other tributes came from Glasgow Celtic, various Celtic supporters' clubs, Glasgow Rangers, Thornwood Rangers Supporters' Club, Ards, Bangor, Glentoran, Linfield, the Irish Football Association and Bangor Supporters' Club.

Among the mourners in the crowded St John's were Caroline Tully (his widow), Charles, Brian and Patricia (his children), Mary Tully (his mother), William, Peter, John and Seamus (his brothers), Nellie, Marie and Kathleen (his sisters) and all of his neighbours in that closely knit community in the Falls Road.

And, lining the route to the Milltown Cemetery, were thousands of ordinary men, women and children paying a last tribute to a local hero – in every sense of the words. A boy who had travelled, won fame if not fortune on the mainland, and who had returned to his roots in the community; a football player, the scorer of the winning goal for Belfast Celtic in the 1947 Irish Cup Final against Glentoran, and a star with the even more famous Glasgow Celtic for a decade; and, to paraphrase Kipling, a man who 'walked with kings and kept the common touch'.

### Note

1. Rafferty omitted to mention Jock Stein's relationship with the troubled Jimmy Johnstone, perhaps the only other player who rivals Charlie Tully in the affections and esteem of the Celtic support.

# Chapter 18
# *The Real Charlie Tully*

Every comedian, it is said, harbours the secret desire to play Hamlet, one of Shakespeare's tragic heroes. Charlie Tully might well be considered the opposite – a prince among players who preferred to play the jester. And such contrariness was entirely in tune with Charlie's character. As shown on the football pitch, any clowning was often a tactic designed to upset opponents. And it worked spectacularly often enough. It was but one weapon in a master player's arsenal, but it is the one most recalled.

Charlie Tully sat on the ball in a game against Rangers. He did not, but he is remembered as having done so. What should be recalled about that particular match on 25 September 1948 is that Charlie Tully could have sat on the ball, so mesmerising and effective had been his performance against the Ibrox side's 'Iron Curtain' defence. It was Charlie Tully performing at Parkhead that afternoon, and not Charlie Chaplin.

The clowning was usually done with intent and more frequently in the closing stages of a match already won. Charlie Tully was a footballer and, despite his extravagant talent, he was making a living in a precarious profession. He did have a showman's instinctive knowledge of how far he could go – in his case in testing the patience and tolerance of referees and in gauging the mood of the thousands on the terracing.

Willie Fernie, who played alongside him often enough, described Tully as 'a master dribbler, very hard to dispossess but, when he passed, he never wasted a ball'. The Celtic Supporters' Association, in its handbook for the following 1958–59 season, paid tribute to the team that had won the League Cup in a lengthy poem; Tully was accurately described:

*Tully, the merry schemer,*

*Dire purpose dressed in glee,*

*Elusive as a leprechaun,*

*Round a fairy thorn tree.*


The football pitch was Charlie Tully's stage, and talent and skill made him the actor in the spotlight. The backing and expectation of an adoring public, the excitement of a big game and the surge of adrenaline all combined to make Charlie Tully feel he had to be centre-stage. Given his natural talent, it would only be normal for Charlie to show off, to delight in the pleasure of the moment. It could become too easy for him to rationalise in his own mind, and why not? *Football is meant to be entertaining, isn't it?* Of course, he overdid things on occasion. However, it is very difficult to pinpoint a particular moment in which a self-indulgent action by Tully actually cost his side the match. Like all players, he did have bad days on which he contributed little to the match or was outplayed by his immediate opponent. On such occasions, he cut a waif-like figure.

A social being, Charlie Tully hated to be alone; he dreaded it. His was a personality that loved company – and to talk about football. Not vainglorious boasting about his own exploits, but discussing the nuances of the sport seriously through detailed analysis of tactics, evaluation of managers and observations on players. Charlie Tully was obsessed with football and, despite what often appeared to be a cavalier approach on the pitch, he was a serious student of the game. A psychiatrist might detect a hint of insecurity in his need for company. Whatever the motivation, Billy McNeill remembers being invited, almost summoned, to 174 Randolph Drive:


*I was a young reserve player at the time, and Charlie was in his last season with*

*Celtic. It was an end-of-season match, and as usual a couple of reserve players travelled with the team to carry the hampers. Mike Jackson and I were picked this time, and Charlie invited us to his house to stay the Saturday night. I think his wife Carrie and the family had gone on ahead back to Belfast. We didn't need to think twice about it — an invite from Charlie Tully! We blethered half the night. It was a great experience for us. We were both star-struck by him — even though he was always pleasant and down-to-earth with us. I considered it a great honour.*[1]

When Tully made that incredible impact in Scotland, against a backdrop of austerity and blandness, he was a journalist's dream: charming, articulate, witty and sharp off the field; brilliant, unpredictable and effective on it. In an age waiting for a character to define it, Charlie Tully represented the player as personality. Football had always been considered a sport and an entertainment, but the entertainment arose mainly through the mastery of skills and a display of those on the football pitch. Charlie Tully added to that his own personal charisma and show business elements.

Football, despite all the pre-game planning and tactics talks, remains a kaleidoscope of infinite improvisation, and it is only the master craftsman who can improvise to devastating effect. Tully was such an improviser. Confident in his own ability, he did not have to plan too far ahead on the football pitch. Johnny Paton remembers the difficulties of partnering him: 'Charlie Tully was a great individualist, not so much a team player. During the war I knew what it was like to play on the left wing alongside great players (such as Malky MacDonald, Len Goulden, Peter Docherty and Stanley Mortensen), but I have to admit I never knew which position to run into when Charlie had the ball; I don't think Charlie himself knew what he was going to do or where he was going to place it.'

It was Tully's conscious unpredictability that he could employ as a tactical ploy, and there was no doubt that he was a master of gamesmanship — defined famously as 'the art of winning without actually cheating but coming very close to it'. Charlie Tully's odd habit of committing the most blatant foul on his immediate opponent in the early minutes of a match was like that. It would never be a nasty offence but perhaps a two-handed shove in the back as his opponent went to head the ball. It would have preyed on the defender's mind for the rest of the game: *is he going to push me again? What will he be up to next?* And, faced with an indecisive opponent, Tully was the man to take full advantage of the situation. He was accused often enough of cheating by such ploys as stealing yards at a throw-in, placing the ball just outside the arc or using his arms while chesting the ball — and, of course, there was the constant chatter.

What did Alf Ramsey, for example, think of his relatively unknown opponent at Windsor Park in 1952? Malcolm Brodie recalls 'Charlie Tully was sometimes in trouble with referees during his Belfast Celtic days but never for rough or dirty play. He used to talk back and make cheeky comments.' Joe Mercer's words come to mind: 'Charlie Tully? Oh yes, Charlie…playing against him was an education in itself!' Bob Crampsey, a most perceptive observer of the Scottish game, points out accurately enough: 'Tully took great delight in seeing how far he could go within the letter of the law. Blessed — or cursed — with native wit, he was quick to see the possibilities within a given situation.' And he recalls the famous situation when Celtic and Third Lanark attempted to play a Scottish Cup tie at Cathkin as a 'friendly' (on a pitch inches deep in snow):

*With 19,000 inside the ground, having paid money to see the Cup tie, the clubs would keep the 'gate' if a friendly was played. It was farcical: within the first few seconds the ball had stuck in the snow, players were slipping and the crowd were*

*starting to get irritated. Charlie Tully was the first player to throw a snowball that day,*
*and the match — which never should have started — was abandoned promptly. And Tully*
*was quite right in showing the absurdity of it all. Charlie was a character straight out*
*of Damon Runyon.*

But the point of all these disconcerting actions was that they were calculated. If Tully got away with anything, it was a matter of celebration and a defeat for repression; if not, he could be looked upon as a victim of an unsympathetic authority. Perhaps his more outrageous antics on the football pitch were motivated by his insecurity, his bravado acting as a form of security blanket.

The 1948–49 season had established Charlie Tully as a star, the most talked about player in Scotland. The following season confirmed his status, but controversy was in the air after the incident at Ibrox with Sammy Cox, the threatened walk-off at Celtic Park, the club suspension and another year out of the major honours for Celtic. At this time the persona — the mask — of Charlie Tully was confirmed. He was widely criticised, and the gamesmanship was construed as cheating. Tully's response was typical: he became a model of politeness, accepting referees' decisions with exaggerated grace, helping up opponents after fouling them and retrieving the ball and placing it for them. All of these actions were, of course, calculated to infuriate further, to distract the opposition even more, and his tactics worked often enough.

Tully's attitude towards training was, like everything else in his football life, contradictory. It has been generally accepted that Charlie Tully disliked the grind of training, as these quotes from contemporaries suggest:

Sean Fallon: *'Charlie Tully hated training; he performed on the pitch. At training he*
*always wanted the ball used — and he was right. He used to lap the track with me at*

*times, and I remember him complaining "Will all this running around the track make you a better player, Sean?"'*

Johnny Paton: *'Charlie Tully was a poor trainer, but he didn't need to work hard at it. He was lightly built and never put on too much weight. Charlie was easy to get along with. I often partnered him at training: jogging, running and sprinting. He was a breath of fresh air. He was full of 'blarney' in a most likeable way.'*

Alec Boden: *'Alec Dowdells was very popular with all the players. He made only occasional appearances to supervise the training; most of his time was spent in treating injured players in the medical room. I suppose Charlie Tully was the bane of his existence. It was left to the player to do his own training and to keep fit himself.'*

One former Celtic player, who prefers to remain unidentified, told me that Charlie Tully and Dick Beattie, (the goalkeeper in the 7–1 side) frequently travelled together to night training sessions at Celtic Park. 'Neither was a good trainer. In fact, Beattie used to buy a fish supper on his way to the ground and on the first lap round the track skipped into "The Jungle" and sat there for most of the session eating his fish-and-chips. We didn't have floodlights in those days, and Charlie used to join him from time to time. The training was a joke.'

Rather surprisingly, in view of his attitude towards the physical work involved in training sessions, Charlie praised Celtic's trainer, Willie Johnstone, in his column in the *Evening Citizen* as 'a hard man at times, bringing us back most afternoons, but he is for us. And we respond by giving him all we've got at training and on the field. Some of the boys actually turned up at Parkhead last Sunday (the day after the 7–1 match)'. This simply does not square with the facts and lends credence to the view that the column, obviously ghostwritten, is not to be taken too seriously as a source of factual information about Celtic.

When Charlie was a youngster on the books of Belfast Celtic, his poor attitude could be interpreted as a teenage rebellion against boring, repetitive physical exercises. Afraid of losing his chance at a football career, he submitted unwillingly to Elisha Scott's regimen (but admitted later that Belfast Celtic were known for finishing matches fresher than their opponents). Established as a star player at Glasgow Celtic, Tully could indulge himself more. Whenever he was seen lapping the track with the other players, the word would spread that Bob Kelly, the ultimate authority at Celtic Park, was in the ground and probably watching the training.

Bobby Murdoch, a keen and enthusiastic teenager at the time, was told by the older hands in 1959 to closely observe Tully's arrival to the team bus as it set out for Seamill for a proposed long-distance run to build up stamina in the pre-season training. He watched carefully:

> Everybody was on the bus, the trainer was looking at his watch, the driver was waiting and Charlie Tully came rushing up from London Road. He was full of apologies; he had been a witness to an accident, and the police had held him up while they took a statement from him about 'some old lady that had fallen off a tram car'. All the older players were in stitches; they knew that Charlie had timed things perfectly, probably keeking round a corner until the bus was ready to go and then racing up to it. He had it figured out that nobody would ask him to go inside the park and get stripped, and hold the bus and everybody up. And he could get away with it! The rest of us would run for miles down at Seamill, and he would just do gentle walking exercises.

The *Sunday Post* of 26 July 1959 reported the matter slightly differently and suggested that player and club, both in two minds about the future, might have conflicting views about the value of 'an eight-mile run from Dalry to Fairlie where they [the players] would re-board the bus. The only exception, a player allowed to stay on the bus for the whole journey, was Charlie Tully, "retained by Celtic but had not re-signed"'. According to the newspaper, he was still training every day with Celtic although he did not take part in both the morning and afternoon sessions which were compulsory for players. But the Celtic players had expected such antics from Charlie and may not have fully realised that the veteran's career as a Celtic player had come to an end.

Of course, Tully was often testing the waters, trying to see just how much he could get away with – and calculating it to a nicety. He had been caught in a role. Such behaviour was expected of him, the so-called 'cheeky chappie', and he did his best to live up to the image. Astute observers suggest that Tully was not as lax in training as he appeared to be; he was a player who knew his physical limitations and did not exceed them, and he was aware of the amount of exercise that would keep him in a reasonable shape. But, typically of the impish Irishman, he preferred to give the impression that he never trained at all. Johnny Paton's words come to mind: 'Charlie was fit – after all, he lasted more than 10 seasons at Celtic Park as a first-team player.'

Charlie Tully could claim accurately that he was the first 'celebrity' player. Others had gained fame through their talent on the pitch and their admirable, totally dedicated professionalism, but Charlie Tully, off the field, was witty and charming, and he could be relied upon to provide a quip or a succinct phrase. His football skill made him the idol of the Celtic support, swollen after his arrival in 1948. To their delight, he was a personality as well, capable of playing to the gallery. In those austere days, he was the type of personality that the times required.

Charlie Tully and Jimmy Johnstone lived out their dreams on their own terms; their performances were definite statements of their personalities. The cult of celebrity seems a new phenomenon throughout an age in which people are famous simply for being famous. Charlie Tully, however, gained fame for being a highly successful footballer. The celebrity status was an extra, deserved because of his talent and engaging personality. However, he did relish the limelight. The *Belfast Telegraph* previewed the Northern Ireland match against France in Paris on 11 November 1952: 'Everywhere Tully goes he is the centre of attention. He walks around wearing dark glasses with a cigarette jutting from an ultra-modern holder. "The Farouk of Paris", the effervescent Eddie McMorran (another Irish internationalist) calls him.'

It went too far, of course, but much of it was not Tully's fault. Reporters vied with each other in reproducing Tullyisms (stories attributed to the player). Older football followers could recognise the hoary chestnuts attributed to the personable Tully and believed by a more gullible younger generation. Annoying and tiresome it may have been, but it was an indication of his stature and fame. After all, apocryphal stories are attributed only to a Winston Churchill and not to a Clement Attlee.

Charlie Tully Jr insists that his father was basically a shy man but felt he had to play a role because it was expected of him. The ready smile, the happy-go-lucky air, the quip and the willingness to sign autographs at length were all produced on cue. According to Charlie Jr, his continuing fame embarrassed him, and he dreaded being praised excessively by strangers. 'Don't get me wrong. My father knew very well that he was a great player and was proud of the contribution that he had made to Celtic, but he still felt a bit awkward deep down about the attention he got in public.'

Skilled at concealing his shyness, Charlie Tully might well have made an excellent pundit on TV or radio. He had the quick wit, a pleasing Irish accent and considerable knowledge of the game. Patricia Conlon, his daughter, points out 'Charlie would often have a lie-down on Sunday afternoons. He would read the papers, all of them, and pore over the football reports. A passion for football, he had.' By all accounts, he could be 'the life and soul of the party' as well – a character trait desirable in the media.

A friend of mine, a sociologist, has suggested that working-class people often exhibit a fear of success and are more comfortable with a form of 'failure'. He qualifies this by suggesting that it may be better described as 'a fear of the unknown or venturing into uncharted social waters.'

If this theory is applied to Charlie Tully, it might well explain some aspects of his character and behaviour. For example, Tully might well have rationalised his dismissive attitude to training as an excuse for any failure or lapse on the football pitch. Similarly, his habit of attempting and failing the outrageous on the pitch, such as the scissor-kick, is understandable because few would have tried it in the first place. If it does not come off, it can hardly be considered a failure. And the same criterion might be applied to the various ploys that earned him the nickname of 'Cheeky Charlie'. If spectators considered him a joker and an entertainer (rather than a mere footballer), he could not be blamed too much.

Even more critically, the same could also be applied to his attitude towards finances and planning for the future. Perhaps, Charlie Tully – and other footballers of that era – recognised subconsciously that long-term success would not be theirs, that their moment in the sun would be fleeting. Most of the ingredients that made up a complex character might well be his stratagems against fate.

In the 1950s class distinctions were more rigid than today. Modern footballers, earning thousands of pounds weekly, cannot be expected to live in the same surroundings and style as their fans. Despite the adulation, footballers of Tully's era could be considered working class in every way – wages, houses, tastes and expectations. Charlie Tully was a prisoner of that mentality; on the football pitch he could express himself as an artist, off it he was expected to conform. And it was difficult not to conform. A new car, a more comfortable home in a better neighbourhood, foreign holidays, stylish clothes and a different accent could all be interpreted as a form of class betrayal; so, the territory of upward mobility was an unknown world for the footballer of the 1950s. It was much easier to remain a part of what was familiar. A psychiatrist might consider that as being pre-conditioned for failure and having a reluctance to grasp fully the possibilities of success. By today's norms it all sounds hopelessly old-fashioned, but it was a fairly prevalent syndrome in those days.

In Charlie Tully's case, it may not have been a reluctance to succeed or an economic death wish; rather it was the fear of the unknown.

Throughout this book Charlie Tully has been put under the microscope as a footballer but only indirectly as a human being. It is time to remedy that, but obituaries have the habit of turning into eulogies in which only praise is bestowed. That may appear the case with Charlie Tully, but the following words are sincere and heartfelt.

*Charlie Tully, recognised universally as a gifted footballer, was also a thoroughly decent man, a good man and a generous man. He gave freely and willingly of his time (and money) to his family, friends and acquaintances throughout his life.*

*In times and circumstances that could have encouraged bitterness and division among Catholics and Protestants in Northern Ireland, he was fair-minded and tolerant. He had the gift of friendship and made friends equally easy on both sides of any religious or social barriers.*

*He will always be remembered as a famous football player with Northern Ireland, Belfast Celtic and Glasgow Celtic but would have been missed as an exemplary family man and a good neighbour. His life as husband and father was a model, and his standing and respect within the community beyond reproach.*

*Any faults or weaknesses, if they have to be pointed out at all, were very human ones: a need for companionship and craic, a restlessness and low tolerance for boredom (perhaps due to hyperactivity), and an unreadiness to plan too far ahead... very human and perhaps very Irish — but not too much there for the scandal sheets and pages of the tabloids.*

*Brilliant and frequently controversial on a football field; decent and respectable off it: Charles Patrick Tully.*

## Note

1. Ironically, Billy McNeill made a point of telling Charlie Jr about this at Charlie Tully's funeral in 1971. 'He [Billy McNeill] told me about the time he was clearing things up after his own father's death and he came across a letter he, as a young reserve player with Celtic, had written — and it was still in the drawer in his father's desk. He had written to his father about the night at Charlie Tully's.' Billy's own account verifies it: 'My father was in the army and stationed in west Africa, and I was just breaking into the reserves at that time. I used to write to keep him up-to-date with everything, and I guess he kept it. He thought that me meeting Charlie was worth remembering.'

# Appendices

## Tullyisms

According to Alec Dowdells, Celtic's trainer, 'The moment Charlie Tully stepped off the Irish boat, somebody pressed a button and the first Charlie Tully story started circulating. Before he was a week at Celtic Park, they were coming off the assembly line faster than Ford cars.' The impact – and the lasting impression – made by Charlie Tully is revealed by the stories and the witticisms attributed to the Irishman. A selection, mercifully short, follows:

Charlie Tully did not need to pay income tax because he had 10 dependants.

———

Celtic visited Rome in 1950, a Holy Year, and were given an audience with Pope Pius XII. Spectators in St Peter's Square were reported as wondering 'Who's the man in the white suit standing beside Charlie Tully?'

———

Tully was recalled, rather surprisingly, to the Northern Ireland team in 1958 at about the time the Pope died. He pointed out that he had seen two newspaper bills, side by side, in the city centre: 'Holy Father Dies In Rome' and 'Tully Gets Another Honour.'

———

Several quotes have been attributed to Tully, and some have the ring of truth:

John McPhail claimed that he used to meet up regularly with Charlie Tully and Tommy McInally 'and the wit of Tommy and Charlie could have filled any Glasgow music hall of the time'. When he was listening to Tommy McInally boast about the pace of the Celtic teams of the 1920s, Tully interrupted to point out 'Of course you're quite right, Tommy, but remember the fastest thing around on the roads then was a horse.'

————

Asked about Celtic's full-backs, Tully responded 'Passable'.

————

Tully used to provide crosses with pin-point accuracy for John McPhail to score with his head. In the early 1950s the balls had to be laced up and were heavy, and McPhail on one occasion mentioned to Tully that he had grazed his forehead with the lace. Charlie quickly apologised: 'Sure now, I must have mistimed the cross.'

————

After Northern Ireland lost heavily to England and he had been largely invisible, Tully pointed out 'Well, I got 10 kicks of the ball: one at the kick-off and the other nine after England scored their goals.'

———

After listening to Bob Kelly and Jimmy McGrory repeatedly telling the story of Patsy Gallacher's famous goal in the 1925 Scottish Cup Final, Tully commented 'Patsy must have started at Melbourne Airport, hopped on to a plane at London, jumped on a helicopter to Hampden Park, grabbed a taxi down the left wing to score the goal; that's the only way he could have passed all the people they claim he passed.'

———

Describing Alf Ramsey, England's right-back: 'My kind of player. He plays like an outside-right; I think he tackles only on Holy Days.'

———

Bantering with Celtic supporters in Lisbon for the 1967 European Cup Final, and asked if he thought he could make the team: 'Sure now, I could take the corners, couldn't I?'

## The Flag Flutter

In 1952 the possibility existed that Celtic might be expelled from football altogether, and Charlie Tully was involved, albeit peripherally, in the situation. On 3 November 1951 Tully was ordered off – the only time in his career – in a humdrum League fixture against Third

Lanark at Celtic Park, when he kicked out at George Aitken. It was the correct decision by the referee, G. Mitchell (Falkirk), but it was greeted with hostility by the crowd, and the match officials met with a stormy reception upon leaving the pitch at the end of the game. One of the linesmen complained later of 'assault by spitting', and this was noted in the referee's report. Subsequently, Celtic were ordered to post warning bills regarding spectators' conduct, and Bob Kelly objected on Celtic's behalf. However, Celtic were informed tartly that 'no evidence other than the linesman's word was required and that a repetition of such conduct may lead to serious action being taken against the club, including possible closure of the ground'.

Two months later Charlie Tully was again the centre of unwanted attention in the traditional Old Firm fixture on 1 January 1952. Early in the second half, with Rangers leading 2–1 on a quagmire of a pitch at Parkhead, he and the Rangers full-back 'Tiger' Shaw clashed, and the Ibrox captain was carried off, unable to return. It seemed as if Tully, in warding off a robustly threatening tackle, had retaliated first. None of the newspapers blamed him – an indication of the respect in which he was held. Trouble broke out on the terracing and grew worse as Rangers went on to win the match by 4–1:

> *The disgraceful behaviour of a small section of the 40,000 crowd at Celtic Park almost succeeded in spoiling the pleasure of the vast majority, who could not possibly have expected to see so exhilarating and so skilful a display of football as both teams – and Rangers in particular – provided on a ground that was a sea of melting snow and mud...It is to the great credit of all of them (the players) that nothing happened on the field which could have been construed as provocative of the hooliganism at the Celtic supporters' end of the ground.*
> (*Glasgow Herald*, 2 January 1952)

Following this disorder, the Glasgow magistrates entered the debate, and that led directly to a prolonged crisis that was termed 'the great flag debate', which raised the possibility of Celtic being banned from competitive football in Scotland. The football authorities, and in particular the SFA, did not want any interference from outside agencies and moved to act. One of the magistrates' recommendations aroused considerable controversy: '…that the two clubs should avoid displaying flags which might incite feeling among the spectators.' This was clearly a specific reference to the flag of Eire, which flew over one end of the covered enclosure – and at the Celtic end of the ground. No doubt it was the source of some irritation among some of Rangers' followers, but it would be difficult to equate the flying of this flag with outbreaks of hooliganism. If the visiting fans had been offended, why had the trouble broken out among Celtic supporters on 1 January 1952? And why had outbreaks occurred in the past at such venues as Ibrox and Hampden, where no such flag had been flown?

When the SFA met to consider the matter in full, attention had switched almost entirely to the issue of the Eire tricolour. Celtic, led by Bob Kelly, were determined to continue flying the flag, considering that it had played no part in disturbances involving Celtic supporters. The SFA, led from behind as always by George Graham, its long-time secretary, seemed determined to humiliate the club as much as possible. The consequences could be earth-shattering if Celtic continued to defy the SFA: a fine, no doubt prohibitive, the closure of Celtic Park (as had happened before), the suspension of Celtic from all organised football…or all of these penalties.

In the end, common sense prevailed, and the SFA withdrew its opposition to Celtic's continued flying of the Eire tricolour – a gesture intended by Celtic to commemorate the historic ties of the club to Ireland.

# Full Circle

Sometimes the progress of a life can appear circular. In a sense, that was the case with Charlie Tully. He was an Irishman, who was born in Belfast in July 1924 and died in Belfast in July 1971, having achieved his greatest fame elsewhere. He was born at 174 McDonnell Street, just off the Falls Road, and died at 9 St James Road, equally close to the Falls Road. Both terraced houses, both in streets adjoining the predominantly Catholic and nationalist Falls Road, and both showing only minimal improvements in the intervening 46 years.

Derek Dougan, in his autobiography, describes his own background in the neighbouring (and not dissimilar) Shankill: 'When I lived on Avon Street, no one, as far as I know, had a bath or running hot water in the house. There was a time when my own father went for his weekly bath to the Public Baths in Templemore Avenue.' The place was much the same, as was the mood: 1924 was a poverty-stricken time, the world fit for heroes had not materialised after World War One, and the unrest caused by the emergence of the Irish Free State was palpable; 1971, even with the introduction of the welfare state, was equally impoverished, and the resumption of 'The Troubles' had only exacerbated the situation. Political unrest, sectarian violence and poverty were the constants of Charlie Tully's life. Hardship was a common factor throughout many of those years. Charlie Tully, despite his enduring claim to fame, never did own a house of his own.

There were compensations. Charlie was the second-born child of a family that eventually totalled 12 and, almost through necessity, was close-knit and supportive. Indeed, the larger community of the Falls Road rallied and stood together in times of hardship. When he died, he and his wife Carrie were raising three children and, as a settled, happy family unit, lived with Carrie's mother and aunt in St James Road.

The two principal football clubs in Charlie Tully's career were Belfast Celtic and Glasgow Celtic, and the parallels between them are striking. Both clubs represented, to a remarkable extent, the hopes and aspirations of an entire community – a deprived Irish and Catholic community within a larger society, which could be viewed as hostile. Both organisations, considering the difficulties they had to endure, were astonishingly successful but aroused resentment as a consequence. Both teams (incidentally sporting identical strips) faced local and intimidating rivals in the form of Linfield and Glasgow Rangers (again wearing virtually identical strips). In each case, accusations, and not just by the two Celtics, were made that their rivals (Linfield in Belfast and Rangers in Glasgow) received preferential treatment from sympathetic authorities in Northern Ireland and Scotland. More importantly, both Celtic teams, from their earliest days, have fielded players chosen on no other basis than their ability and willingness to play football; in a similar way, the most celebrated managers of both clubs (Elisha Scott and Jock Stein) have been non-Catholics. Unfortunately, their rivals, for a considerable period of time, chose to exercise a ban on Catholic players – and this action served to add a further dimension to the football tension and rivalry between the clubs, as well as doing nothing to decrease sectarian hostility in the general community.

In 1949, only a year after Charlie Tully left them, Belfast Celtic went out of existence, largely as a consequence of the hostility they faced within Ulster. In 1952, only four years after he joined them, Glasgow Celtic came close to being expelled from membership of the SFA (and the Scottish League) because of bigotry within the offices of the SFA, in the person of its long-time secretary George Graham (later knighted for 'services to football').

## Last Word

Glen Daly ('Half Irish, Half Scots, Half Daft', according to his stage billing) is credited with writing *The Celtic Song*, still sung enthusiastically by the thousands at Celtic Park almost 50 years on. The singer has recounted that he had considerable difficulty in coming up with the words of the second verse and, only an hour or so before recording it at Pye Studios in London, he recalled a version:

> *We don't care if we win, lose or draw,*
> *Darn the hair we care.*
> *Because we only know that there's*
> *Going to be a show*
> *And the Glasgow Celtic will be there.*

Those were the words he settled on, and he remembered where he had first heard them sung: in the Kenilworth Hotel in Glasgow, sung by a certain Charles Patrick Tully, who claimed that a similar version had been sung regularly in Belfast to cheer on another Celtic.

The music and the memories live on…